THE
PLANT LOVER'S GUIDE
TO
EPIMEDIUMS

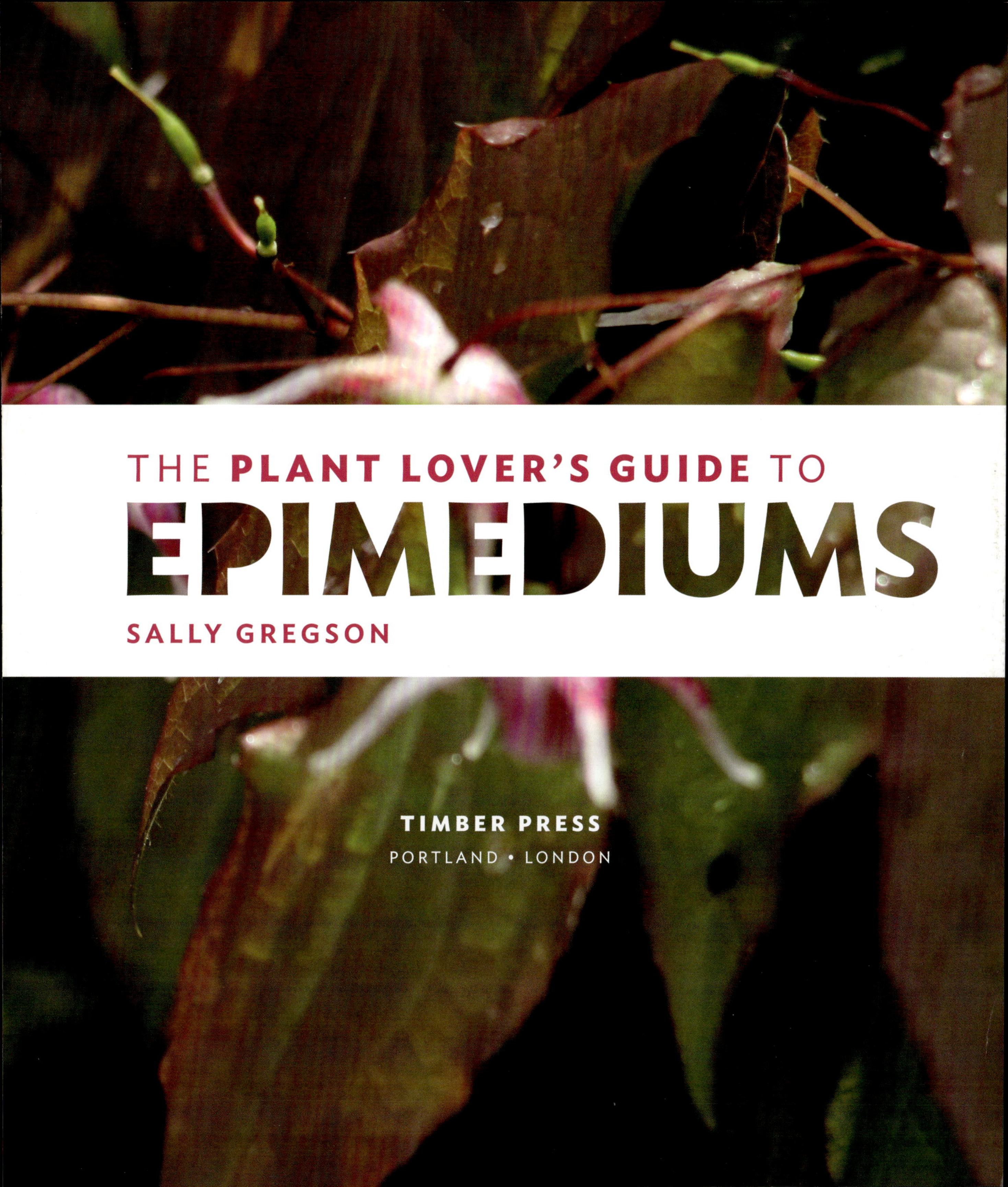

THE PLANT LOVER'S GUIDE TO
EPIMEDIUMS

SALLY GREGSON

TIMBER PRESS
PORTLAND · LONDON

CONTENTS

6
Why I Love Epimediums

11
Designing with Bishop's Hats, Barrenworts, and Fairy Wings

47
123 Epimediums for the Garden

173
Growing and Propagating

197
People, Places, and Plants

WHERE TO BUY 222
WHERE TO SEE 224
FOR MORE INFORMATION 226
HARDINESS ZONE
TEMPERATURES 228
ACKNOWLEDGEMENTS 229
PHOTO CREDITS 230
INDEX 231
ABOUT THE AUTHOR 238

WHY I LOVE EPIMEDIUMS

If you think of epimediums as quiet, useful little plants for dry shade, you haven't seen the newly discovered species from China and their exciting hybrids.

These showgirls, as I like to call them, lend an ethereal air to woodland gardens and grow well in most soils. In fact, more and more professional garden designers are placing groups of epimediums among other spring-flowering bulbs and plants to achieve a tapestry of colour and texture. Chinese epimediums are astonishing. They are new to most Western gardeners, and they have started a revolution in the horticultural world.

Easy-to-grow, undemanding epimediums contribute handsome evergreen foliage and elegant flowers to the garden. Some of these species have large blossoms that resemble hang-gliding spiders suspended above brightly splashed and marbled young leaves. Others have clouds of small starry flowers like pale moths in flight. Still others have dainty cup-shaped bells on thin wiry stems. I love them all. Their floral colours vary from white and pale yellow to pink, purple, brown, and red. Some flowers are bi-coloured; others have spurs with contrasting tips. Several species save their hues for their especially remarkable young foliage.

Epimedium pubescens growing in the wild in Dujiangyan, Sichuan.

Let me backtrack for a minute. As a gardener, nursery owner, and garden writer, I often come across new forms of favourite old plants at flower shows and plant fairs. Every spring brings forth a new crop of must-have botanical stars. But occasionally a species unfamiliar to Western horticulture emerges from a plant-hunting expedition to an unvisited, unexploited part of the world. Twenty years ago Chinese epimediums were such a novelty. Their arrival heralded not just one or two species, but a deluge of new varietals from the provinces of Sichuan and Yunnan.

Surprisingly, the gardening world did not change overnight. Many gardeners have continued to grow the epimediums they already knew, such as *Epimedium pinnatum*, *E.* ×*perralchicum* 'Fröhnleiten', and various selections of *E. grandiflorum*. Most of us thought we understood them all. I know I did.

Then one day I visited the now-defunct Washfield Nursery in Kent, England, which was run by Elizabeth Strangman. While browsing among the treasures, I found a cache of rather different epimediums. One that immediately caught my eye was *Epimedium* 'Enchantress', a totally new form I had never seen. Its lavender buds opened to palest

Old favourite *Epimedium grandiflorum* 'Lilafee' grows well in acid soil and dies back in a blaze of autumn glory to re-emerge in spring with a flourish. Its bright rose pink flowers make up for their small size by appearing en masse.

grey-lavender petals that deepened to purple, and its long-toothed young leaves had crimson spots and splashes. It was a world away from my experience of the old familiar epimediums growing in a shady rockery in my garden.

Upon witnessing my fascination with 'Enchantress', Elizabeth suggested that I visit Robin White's Blackthorn Nursery in Hampshire, England. There I encountered *Epimedium franchetii* 'Brimstone Butterfly', which stole the show with its large-spurred primrose yellow flowers suspended above long bronze-pink young leaves. As more epimediums began appearing in small specialist nurseries, I began to collect them with enthusiasm. My eyes were opened. I was completely hooked.

One of the things that amazed me about these plants was their diversity of colours, shapes, and sizes. There were myriad possibilities to add to my burgeoning collection, from pale pink *Epimedium acuminatum* through pure white *E. ogisui* to caramel brown *E. wushanense* 'Caramel', with spidery flower shapes floating on wiry stems above red-splashed and spotted young leaves, or dainty spurless caps in vivid pink or yellow. The new epimediums were an Aladdin's cave of jewels that introduced novelty into my garden.

As I collected epimediums, I took time to learn about the modern-day plant-hunters who introduced them, as well as the places where the plants were found. I heard stories of deep, dark valleys in China, each with its own population of one or two species. Within each valley those species had inter-bred and produced natural hybrids. One of the new plants I acquired at this time bore the name *Epimedium ×omeiense* 'Emei Shan'

The lovely *Epimedium ×omeiense* 'Akane', a naturally occurring hybrid, has large red in-curved petals with yellow-tipped spurs and golden mouth above young leaves splashed with bronze spots.

(now *E.* ×*omeiense* 'Akane') after the sacred Buddhist mountain where it was gathered. I learned about Emei Shan (Mount Omei) and was captivated by the thought of thousands of pilgrims dutifully climbing their way up steep steps and pathways to get closer to the 3000 m (10,000 ft.) peak to catch a glimpse of the "Buddha Light." This curious effect is glimpsed when the peak is shrouded in cloud. At dawn the shadow of each visitor is silhouetted against the nebula surrounded by a circular rainbow like a halo. The spectrum of colour is reflected at their feet in the flowers of multiple epimediums, not least *E.* ×*omeiense* 'Akane' itself.

Alongside the epimediums, I planted *Corydalis solida*, *C. flexuosa*, *Helleborus* ×*hybridus*, *Bergenia* species and cultivars, and *Dicentra formosa*. The epimediums grow under roses and shrubs, beneath hydrangeas, and between winter-bright red-stemmed dogwoods. Here they increase gently without getting out of hand, and they contribute not just exquisite flowers but also beautiful foliage. Most of them are evergreen and thus have a presence throughout the year, while the herbaceous forms colour well in autumn before their leaves die back.

Elsewhere in my garden, clumps of *Epimedium* ×*versicolor* 'Sulphureum' frolic in the shade of a weeping birch. Together with *E. pinnatum* subsp. *colchicum* these classic forms never fail to lift my winter spirits with their rafts of chestnut brown foliage, and in spring their demure yellow flowers make me smile. My steadily increasing collection of lime-hating *E. grandiflorum* and *E.* ×*youngianum* is housed in clay pots filled with ericaceous compost and placed beneath a pergola, where the plants enjoy sunshine in spring and are shaded during the summer.

The huge influx of new varieties is exciting and, at times, confusing. In this book, acid-lovers are separated from plants that thrive in dry shade, while the new Chinese species and their hybrids and cultivars, which grow in any shaded soil, are mentioned separately. The plant descriptions, however, are listed alphabetically by the plant's botanical name. The list is by no means comprehensive (nor are the lists of suggested plants for various situations). Rather, I have chosen readily available plants in the United Kingdom, the United States, and Australia.

Epimediums are easy and hardy in the right conditions, and they mainly flower in spring. All make good companions to a jewel box of spring bulbs and early herbaceous perennials. Epimediums are poised to take the gardening world by storm. I hope this book will inspire you to try some of these wonderful plants in your garden.

Epimedium 'Black Sea' with snowdrops and red-stemmed dogwoods in my garden.

DESIGNING WITH BISHOP'S HATS, BARRENWORTS, AND FAIRY WINGS

Hosta, epimedium, and aconite foliage combine in a shady garden.

All epimediums, not just the newly discovered species and hybrids, combine effectively with a host of other shade-loving perennials to create an understorey of plants beneath shrubs, roses, and light garden trees, or below a pergola smothered in clematis and roses. The range of available epimediums includes those that gardeners are accustomed to growing in awkward, dry places in shade; those whose leaves turn copper-bronze for winter decoration; those that are more suited to acid soils; and the huge influx of new species from China and, increasingly, their exciting hybrids.

Garden designers in general still use old favourites, such as *Epimedium pinnatum* subsp. *colchicum*, that cavort in the inauspicious surroundings of dry shade. There are many reasons to stick with tried-and-true epimediums. They are foolproof and will grow in almost any conditions. They are handy for garden owners who have little time for tending and simply want a beautiful outdoor space in which to entertain their friends. Using plants with a known history is a great way to minimize maintenance needs, but this practice also limits variety and interest.

British garden designer Dan Pearson, revered for his plant knowledge, is occasionally asked to use more interesting plants in a garden. He tests his favourite novelties prior to planting them in clients' gardens. Pearson and other garden designers are discovering that even the new epimediums are easy plants and amenable to most soils in bright shade. He recommends *Epimedium acuminatum*, *E. wushanense* 'Caramel', *E.* 'Heavenly Purple', and *E. ×omeiense* 'Akane', and has found that these plants and about a dozen others are reliable performers in gardens and certainly please his clients.

Both the newer epimediums and the older ones bring interesting flower shapes and colourful foliage to a garden. Let's look at some of the possibilities for your space.

Flowers

To watch the first *Epimedium* shoots slowly unfurl free of the blanket of winter leaves is to relish the excitement of anticipation. The buds extend on brittle stems, until one morning a flower reveals itself to the spring sunshine. This is a moment to savour.

Epimedium flowers can vary in size, shape, and colour. They seem fragile and are small at first, but they get bigger as they begin to open, some expanding to the dimensions of a big coin. The larger-flowering forms resemble spiders caught in mid-spin as they spiral down on wiry stems. And the smaller-flowered plants, often daintier in their dimensions, can show a strong will to live.

Parts of an *Epimedium* flower

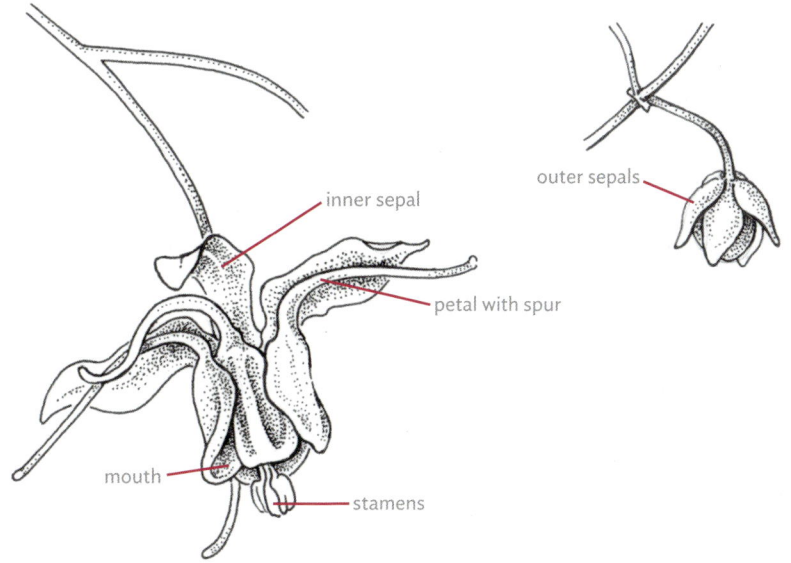

THE FLOWERS OF GROUND-COVERING PLANTS

Epimediums that cover the ground and romp happily in dry shade fulfil a difficult role with character. They produce carpets of two-tone cream and primrose yellow flowers that bring a dark, dry corner of the garden to life in spring. Their usefulness lies in their enthusiasm for populating such dreary, thirsty corners, but sometimes they can become too energetic and require corralling. All you need to control them is a garden spade and a strong back.

Many common forms of epimediums have shining mahogany leaves in winter, followed by cheerful open-eyed yellow flowers in spring. These blooms are worth a closer look. *Epimedium* ×*perralchicum* 'Fröhnleiten' has bright yellow flowers over new young leaves that start red with green veining. Its sunny disposition brings cheer to a cold spring day. It is very similar to *E. pinnatum* subsp. *colchicum*, which is more of a mouthful to say but slightly less domineering in the garden. It has small coral-red central petals that set off the yellow sepals even better.

Epimedium ×*versicolor* 'Neosulphureum' produces numerous flowers, followed by new red leaves in spring. The flowers of the newer *E.* ×*versicolor* 'Cherry Tart' have deep pink sepals over red petals with a distinct yellow eye at the throat. This cultivar has slightly less ardour than 'Neosulphureum' and is readily available from most garden centres and nurseries. *Epimedium* ×*warleyense* has attractive light orange flowers and is slightly less bouncy.

Epimedium ×*perralchicum* 'Fröhnleiten' with foxglove (*Digitalis ferruginea*) and coral bells (*Heuchera* 'Ebony and Ivory') in a mixed border at the Intersection Garden, Witan Street, RHS Garden Wisley.

Epimedium ×*versicolor* 'Neosulphureum', an old-fashioned classic for dry shade, has rounded lemon yellow sepals above small yellow bells with no spurs.

SMALLER-FLOWERED FORMS

Epimedium ×rubrum has dark red flowers that are small but still make quite an impact in the garden. Epimediums with daintier flowers can catch the light like bright flashes of sunshine. *Epimedium davidii*, for example, can illuminate a dark corner with its clouds of butter yellow flowers on red stems and sepals, plus long yellow spurs.

Like moonshine on a clear night, the flowers of *Epimedium* 'Black Sea' are palest cream with splashes of pink against the dark winter foliage. This might be reason enough not to cut back the over-wintered leaves.

The starry white flowers of *Epimedium brevicornu* scintillate with their clean yellow eyes and prominent stamens. They seem like the essence of spring over apple green young leaves. *Epimedium stellulatum* 'Wudang Star' is similar, but with big white sepals and just a hint of cream in its small petals. Any of these would give a true woodland feel under shrubs or light trees.

The bell-shaped flowers of *Epimedium campanulatum* are charming. The small sulphur yellow bells hang down from thin, wiry stems, backed by tiny upstanding white sepals. Closer examination of these blooms will be rewarded. *Epimedium diphyllum* has a similar bell shape but is loosely semi-double and white, like a beautiful old woman with tousled hair.

Epimedium platypetalum has more open four-petalled flowers with little white sepals in a delicate creamy yellow. The flowers are widely open, innocent of the merest hint of

Epimedium davidii shines out in a shaded corner.

Epimedium stellulatum 'Wudang Star' with bright white sepals, yellow petals, and pink-beige young leaves.

Small-flowered Epimediums

Epimedium 'Black Sea'
Epimedium brevicornu
Epimedium campanulatum
Epimedium davidii
Epimedium dolichostemon
Epimedium ecalcaratum
Epimedium fargesii
Epimedium 'Pink Elf'
Epimedium platypetalum
Epimedium ×*rubrum*
Epimedium stellulatum 'Wudang Star'

Epimedium grandiflorum var. *higoense* 'Confetti' produces clouds of white flowers.

Epimedium 'Pink Elf' flowers prolifically in early spring and often repeats the performance at the end of the summer.

a spur. Not so *E. ecalcaratum*, which has very slight spurs on the petals. The black stems seem to set off the cowslip yellow flowers, which are like little box-shaped beads on a fine thread.

The blossoms of *Epimedium fargesii* and *E. dolichostemon* have petals swept back like cyclamen or American cowslip (*Dodecatheon meadia*). Both are small and pale pink, the former with bright purple lips to the central mouth, the latter with small deep purple petals overshadowed by white sepals. These bright little flowers have a vernal innocence to their enthusiasm.

For sheer energy it would be hard to beat *Epimedium* 'Pink Elf'. This small plant runs the risk of flowering itself to death in its eagerness to produce showers of two-tone pink flowers. It blooms almost continuously throughout spring and into summer.

MEDIUM-SIZE FLOWERS

The flower of *Epimedium grandiflorum*, which loves acidic soil, has a distinctive box shape and spurred petals. The new selections are increasingly brightly coloured in shades of pink, violet, and purple. Some clean white varieties glisten like raindrops in the shade, such as *E. grandiflorum* 'White Queen' or lovely *E. grandiflorum* var. *higoense* 'Confetti', which has long white uptilted sepals.

Epimedium grandiflorum 'Lilafee' is an old hybrid created by German hardy-perennial enthusiast Ernst Pagels. It has typical medium rose-purple flowers and is readily available in nurseries. More sought after is *E. grandiflorum* 'Queen Esta', which has larger pink flowers with long white spurs on its petals. The shorter-growing *E. grandiflorum* 'Sirius' has pale rose pink flowers held horizontally above the emerging foliage.

Purple flowers are also quite common in this species. *Epimedium grandiflorum* 'Purple Prince' has perhaps the richest hue, and would make a good companion for its more delicately toned siblings. Likewise, *E. sempervirens* 'Violet Queen' has medium-size flowers in a rich, light purple.

Epimedium 'Alabaster' is a useful and very beautiful plant that is similar in many ways to a white form of *E. grandiflorum*, but it appears not to need acid soil and grows steadily and well. Its light green leaves set off snow white flowers, which are backed by small purple-pink sepals.

Epimedium sempervirens is less widely grown and bred, likely because its flowers are sometimes partially obscured by the young new leaves before they power up over their heads, but new selections hold their flower heads higher and are worthy of a place in an acidic border. This Japanese endemic species requires acidic, draining soil in light shade, but it is, as its name suggests, evergreen.

For spanking white flowers, *Epimedium sempervirens* 'Okuda's White' is unsurpassed. The leaves are light apple green and set off the flowers well. *Epimedium sempervirens* 'Candy Hearts' has large pink flowers that nestle among light green leaves with a coral-pink margin, and *E. sempervirens* 'Mars' is a startling shade of cranberry purple, with distinct white-tipped spurs.

Epimedium ×*youngianum*, the hybrid between *E. diphyllum* and *E. grandiflorum*, inherits a preference for acidic

Epimedium sempervirens 'Okuda's White' sparkles in the shade.

The tousled pale pink flowers of *Epimedium* ×*youngianum* 'Tamabotan' are borne on dark purple stems.

soil, is herbaceous, and has flowers in colours similar to those of *E. grandiflorum*, but some have fewer or no spurs on the petals. *Epimedium ×youngianum* 'Merlin' has distinctive rounded flowers without spurs in a bright cerise that sparkles amid its re-emerging leaves. This wizard seems not to wear a pointed hat. *Epimedium ×youngianum* 'Tamabotan' has small, pendulous palest pink flowers that contrast dramatically with the plant's purple young foliage.

The flowers of *Epimedium membranaceum* are a similar size, but quite different in shape. They have butter yellow spurs and small white sepals. These sparkle. They dance and fizz in the shadows. The light seems to tumble from the flowers, and the whole plant seizes your attention.

LARGER FLOWERS

The category of larger flowers includes the vast realm of the hybrids, as well as some of the newly discovered Chinese species. These blossoms are the stars of spring, and they require careful positioning if you want to enjoy their many charms. They grow better within a defined garden rather than as part of a wilder woodland understorey. These flowers are spectacular and demand attention, so plant them at the front of the border, and be sure their immediate companions set them off rather than rival them. It helps to find a place for them in a shady border where their colours and bi-colours can suggest toning companions.

The large white flowers of *Epimedium* 'Amanogawa' tower over the purplish flowers of *Anemonella thalictroides* f. *rosea* 'Oscar Schoaf'.

White is magical in dappled shade. It gleams like moonlight on silver. It advances out of the penumbra and seizes your attention. However, when planted in quantity, white demands a flash of strongly contrasting colour from another epimedium or from neighbouring woodlanders.

Some epimediums are pure cotton white, while others, such as *Epimedium* 'Arctic Wings', have just a hint of pink. This form stands out as a remarkable new hybrid with clusters of large flowers held facing down, their faces demure. The chalk white is set off by small smoky pink outer sepals that are always visible. *Epimedium ogisui* has pure white leggy blooms. The spring foliage is bronzed and the whole plant shines out of a shady corner. It flowers early in spring, just as the snowdrops begin to fade. *Epimedium* 'Amanogawa' has showers of white blossoms with small central petals in an undefinable yellowish brown.

Pale pastel pink is a pretty, comfortable colour, redolent of rose-scented soap and little girls' tutus. It also shines out of a shady border, and is undemanding, easy, and safe. And there are plenty of pink-flowered epimediums from which to choose.

For simple single-coloured flowers, *Epimedium brachyrrhizum* stands out. Its selection 'Elfin Magic' has delicate pink flowers, thin sepals, and in-curved petals. But the majority of pink-flowered hybrids are bi-coloured. *Epimedium* 'Buckland Spider' has pink-purple sepals above paler pink-spurred petals, streaked and margined white. *Epimedium leptorrhizum* 'Mariko' has long medium pink sepals over equally long white spurs. The stamens extend well below the flower to reveal primrose yellow anthers.

Quite different, but with a similar combination of colours, is *Epimedium* 'Pink Champagne', which has pale pink bubbles of flowers with in-curved spurred petals that deepen to a deep wine-pink in the centre. They are carried above purple-black spotted leaves that create a sombre backdrop for the flowers. The whole plant makes a striking composition.

Epimedium acuminatum commands attention wherever it grows. It carries sprays of pink-sepalled flowers with rich purple petals at the mouth that fade to pink on the spurs. They give the busy appearance of

Large-flowered Epimediums

Epimedium acuminatum 'Night Mistress'
Epimedium 'Amanogawa'
Epimedium 'Arctic Wings'
Epimedium brachyrrhizum
Epimedium chlorandrum
Epimedium epsteinii
Epimedium 'Fire Dragon'
Epimedium grandiflorum 'Queen Esta'
Epimedium 'King Prawn'
Epimedium leptorrhizum 'Mariko'
Epimedium ogisui
Epimedium ×*omeiense* 'Stormcloud'
Epimedium 'Pink Champagne'

The dark-spotted leaves of *Epimedium* 'Pink Champagne' set off the pink flowers.

The flowers of *Epimedium acuminatum* contrast lavender and purple.

Epimedium epsteinii bears plump flowers of purple and white.

clouds of butterflies hovering over the leaves. Something as spectacular as *E. acuminatum* 'Night Mistress', with large sepals above long-spurred bright purple petals and well-marked new leaves, is enough to throw its neighbours into a flurry.

Epimedium 'Enchantress', the early hybrid that Elizabeth Strangman found, is still one of the loveliest bi-coloured forms. The sepals are a soft lavender-pink and the mouth of the petals has a purple margin. *Epimedium* 'Phoenix' is similarly coloured but has slightly darker petals and rich purple buds. The flowers are set amid re-emerging foliage that is long, pointed, and spectacularly splashed with red.

More dramatic still are the flowers of *Epimedium epsteinii*. They have large white sepals and deep purple-brown spurred petals. The whole flower tilts slightly upwards and looks at you through its lashes.

Gold is the colour of sunshine. Sulphur is moonlight. Both reflect more light than any other colour and thus illuminate the shadows. Many modern gardeners still have a pronounced aversion to yellow in both flowers and variegated foliage. However, within the group of large-flowered epimediums, yellow flowers can be pale, interesting, and ethereal or bright, effervescent, and twinkling. Each has its own appealing character.

Epimedium chlorandrum is a subtle combination of lime green, cream, and sulphur yellow. Its large flowers are the size of primroses. The combination of sulphur yellow and white or cream is even more defined in *E.* 'Egret'. It bears big flowers with large white up-swept sepals over clean sulphur petals with long spurs held well above the mottled leaves. And *E. franchetii* 'Brimstone Butterfly' is a symphony of large lemon and sulphur flowers poised like the eponymous insect over bronze-pink foliage. These blooms definitely capture and hold the attention.

One of the original plants collected on Mount Omei was the beautiful bi-colour *Epimedium* ×*omeiense* 'Akane'. Its colouring is similar to the new hybrid *E*. 'Fire Dragon', which has paler coral sepals over lighter yellow petals with long spurs. The latter has the advantage of flowering throughout spring and into early summer.

True red is a rare hue in the world of epimediums. There is more than a trace of ruby red in *Epimedium* 'William Stearn'. Its sepals and upper petals are the colour of ruby port and have long yellow-tipped spurs. The flower does Stearn credit. The modern hybrid *E*. 'Marco' has similar colouring, and either plant would stand out in a terra-cotta pot, where its subtle colours would show well. In the ground the plants need carefully chosen companions to set off the dark red flowers.

Beige, bronze, and apricot merge well and effectively in both the garden and in a terra-cotta pot. Peter Chappell at Spinners Garden and Nursery in Hampshire, England, selected two outstanding forms with these colours: *Epimedium* 'Jean O'Neill' in shades of apricot and coffee, and *E*. 'Spinners' in soft cream and brown. These light-coloured combinations show up well against bare, dark soil in spring. The flowers of *E*. 'Spinners' have cream sepals over long beige petals with in-curved claws that seem to have been dipped in egg yolk. The whole plant grows to 1 m (40 in.), and its foliage makes quite an impression in the garden.

In one or two special selections, beige burns to toffee and amber colours. *Epimedium* 'Amber Queen' is especially well named, as is *E. wushanense* 'Caramel', whose flowers seem to have been dunked in burnt sugar. *Epimedium* ×*omeiense* 'Stormcloud' is a fascinating combination of browns and purples.

The sulphur and white flowers of *Epimedium* 'Egret'.

Epimedium 'Jean O'Neill' has flowers the colour of coffee and cream.

The ruby red flowers of *Epimedium* 'William Stearn'.

The gold and vermilion flowers of *Epimedium* 'Fire Dragon'.

The creamy yellow flowers of *Epimedium wushanense* 'Caramel' appear to have been dipped in toffee.

Foliage

While flowers are pretty, they are also ephemeral and evanescent, whereas a plant's leaves are present for most of the time and contribute form, colour, and structure to the border. Gardening guru Beth Chatto understands this principle well, and has made her mark on the horticultural world by selecting plants with contrasting foliage and form to grow in her garden in the cold, dry soils of Essex, England. She chooses plants with contrasting foliage and form to enrich her plantings, and many forms of *Epimedium* bring handsome leaves in a range of colours, be they evergreen or herbaceous, to join the party.

The widely grown *Epimedium* ×*perralchicum* 'Fröhnleiten', *E. pinnatum* subsp. *colchicum*, and *E.* ×*versicolor* 'Sulphureum' have all proved themselves to be very useful weed-suppressing ground-cover for dry shade. But they also contribute bronze foliage in winter, as well as pretty yellow flowers, and their emerging young leaves in spring are often well marked with rich red veining. Most of the forms of *E.* ×*versicolor* also have brilliantly coloured young leaves.

Epimediums and rodgersias at Wildside in Devon, England.

Evergreen Epimediums

Epimedium 'Buff Beauty'
Epimedium 'Egret'
Epimedium franchetii 'Brimstone Butterfly'
Epimedium 'Honeybee'
Epimedium 'King Prawn'
Epimedium 'Lemon Zest'
Epimedium 'Marco'
Epimedium ×*omeiense* 'Akane'
Epimedium 'Phoenix'
Epimedium 'Pink Champagne'
Epimedium 'Red Maximum'
Epimedium sagittatum 'Warlord'
Epimedium sempervirens 'Violet Queen'
Epimedium 'Space Wagon'
Epimedium 'Spine Tingler'
Epimedium 'Spinners'
Epimedium stellulatum 'Wudang Star'
Epimedium 'The Giant'
Epimedium 'William Stearn'

A curved pathway at Chanticleer Garden in eastern Pennsylvania winds through ground-covering plants that include *Epimedium* ×*versicolor* 'Sulphureum', *Astilbe* 'Deutschland', ostrich fern (*Matteuccia struthiopteris*), and *Viburnum sieboldii*.

The red and green spring foliage of epimediums complements that of variegated fairy bells (*Disporum sessile* 'Variegatum').

Among the plants that associate on a more democratic level are one or two with especially well-coloured winter foliage. The young leaves of *Epimedium brachyrrhizum*, for example, are shaded in surprisingly pastel lilac. Evergreen *E.* 'Black Sea', as its name suggests, has dark green foliage that turns through deep red-maroon to a glossy near-black in a cold winter. This useful specimen has found a home in my own garden between the sealing-wax red stems of ornamental dogwood (*Cornus alba* 'Sibirica') and the winter red leaves of *Bergenia* 'Overture'. In spring, a lime green oriental hellebore takes over from the pruned-down stems of the dogwood, and in the summer the epimedium makes a green petticoat for neighbouring *Hydrangea macrophylla* 'Merveille Sanguine', with its mahogany-brown leaves and red flowers. The whole scheme continues year after year, with only a little weeding and cutting back of stems and leaves in their season.

The spring leaves of Keith Wiley's hybrid *Epimedium* 'Wildside Ruby' are among the most strongly coloured of all. They are deep claret red that perfectly sets off the sparkling pink-and-yellow flowers.

Although *Epimedium grandiflorum* is herbaceous, it dies away in autumn in a blaze of glory and then returns the following spring with fresh green young leaves. Many of its selections, such as 'Bandit', have a distinct black margin to the young leaves that gradually turns to green during the summer. The effect is dramatic.

> ### Epimediums for Fall Foliage Colour
>
> *Epimedium* 'Black Sea'
> *Epimedium* 'Enchantress'
> *Epimedium grandiflorum* and forms
> *Epimedium pinnatum* subsp. *colchicum* 'Thunderbolt'
> *Epimedium* ×*rubrum*
> *Epimedium* ×*versicolor* 'Cherry Tart'
> *Epimedium* ×*youngianum* 'Merlin'
> *Epimedium* ×*youngianum* 'Purple Heart'

Flowers and young foliage on *Epimedium* 'Wildside Ruby'.

Winter leaves on *Epimedium* 'Black Sea'.

The relatively new *Epimedium grandiflorum* 'Dark Beauty' has especially dark brown-purple new foliage.

Iridescent spines edge the salmon-coloured spring leaves of the Chinese species *Epimedium lishihchenii*.

Young leaves of *Epimedium grandiflorum* var. *higoense* 'Bandit' in front of Welsh poppies (*Papaver cambricum*).

Ogisu's form of *Epimedium wushanense* growing beneath *Viburnum tinus*.

The foliage of many of the Chinese species is remarkable in both summer and winter, and the evergreen leaves of Japanese plant-hunter Mikinori Ogisu's form of *Epimedium wushanense* are exceptional. They can be up to 30 cm (12 in.) long, and the whole plant is on an entirely different scale to its brothers and sisters. Not only are the leaves long and spiny, but when they appear in spring they are splashed maroon. Some leaves are entirely crimson, while others are streaked and spotted. The plant would fill a 1-m (40-in.) wide space in the border within a couple of years.

Many breeders of the new hybrids choose primarily plants with especially dramatic young leaves to accompany larger flowers. Because the foliage is present year-round, it is as important as the quality of the flowers.

Epimedium ×*versicolor* behind *Hosta* 'Great Expectations' and *H.* 'June' in a garden in Somerset, England.

Companion Plants

When it comes to designing the planting of your garden, it helps to separate the different types of epimediums according to their soil tolerances and preferences. The following sections deal with companion plants for year-round foliage interest, dry shade, acidic soil, and dappled shade where the soil is fertile and drains off surplus moisture.

PLANTING SCHEMES FOR YEAR-ROUND FOLIAGE

Most of the new Chinese species of *Epimedium* and their hybrids have especially dramatic young foliage that contributes colour, form, and texture to the border throughout the summer and into the winter. They combine well with other plants that feature foliage to create a tapestry of texture and colour throughout the year.

Hostas are the classic large-leaved plants for shade, albeit ambrosia for slugs. If you can work out a slug-and-snail solution that suits your garden, hostas are easily the best foliage companions for the large-leaved epimediums, as well as for many other plants with good spring foliage.

Hardy geraniums are usually grown for their flowers, but the leaves of *Geranium phaeum* 'Samobor' have a distinct black central splash and work well in shade. Many lungworts (*Pulmonaria*) also display well-marked leaves throughout the year, making a good contrast to the foliage of any of the evergreen epimediums. And many of the little woodland bleeding hearts (*Dicentra*) have grey foliage accompanying their heart-shaped flowers in all shades of pink, which makes a softly pretty contrast.

Recently, larger-growing heucheras with proportionately bigger leaves than earlier varieties have been

introduced to the gardening public. Many of these plants rival hostas for their usefulness in contrasting foliage effects. The closely related foamflowers (*Tiarella*) are also evergreen and even tolerate dry shade.

Carol Clements gardens on the heavy alkaline soils of Somerset, England, where some of her borders are beginning to benefit both from the shade of the trees she has planted and those of her neighbours. At the front of her house a shady path is perfect for foliage plants. Here ginger-leaf false bugbane (*Beesia calthifolia*), with its kidney-shaped shiny leaves that turn bronze in a cold winter, grows alongside low, elegant *Hacquetia epipactis* 'Thor', which emerges from dormancy very early in spring with cream-edged leaves, followed by pale yellow flowers whose bracts are similarly edged with cream. These grow alongside *Epimedium ogisui*, whose foliage and white flowers make good companions. In the borders at the back of the house, Clements grows *E.* ×*versicolor*—not just for its dainty spring flowers, but primarily for its coloured foliage in early summer. It makes a long-lasting splash with the young leaves of autumn-flowering monkshood (*Aconitum napellus*) and variegated fairy bell (*Disporum sessile* 'Variegatum').

An attractive combination of *Epimedium* (lower right), an unnamed white-spotted pulmonaria (upper right), brown-spotted *Podophyllum versipelle* 'Spotty Dotty' (upper left), and pink-flowered *Dicentra* 'Stuart Boothman' (lower left) in late spring.

Epimedium ogisui greets visitors with its handsome foliage.

Foliage colour in Carol Clements' spring garden. Note how the colour of the Japanese maple leaves brings out the hue of the epimediums. Monkshood (*Aconitum napellus*) and variegated fairy bell (*Disporum sessile* 'Variegatum') complete the vignette.

PLANTING SCHEMES FOR DRY SHADE

Many woodland plants flower in spring. Deciduous woodland is the natural flora of many parts of northern Europe, the United States, and Australia. Before the trees can grow a canopy to obscure the woodland floor, the winter and spring sunshine permeates the network of overhead branches. A large percentage of English native plants, in particular, emerge from the soil, open their flowers, are pollinated while the light is visible, and set seed as the canopy comes into leaf. Light is then obscured, and there are fewer flowers in summer. Epimediums are therefore wonderful gems for deciduous woodlands.

Epimedium ×*rubrum* does not spread too much in dry shade, but with a little goodness in the soil it makes quite hefty clumps fairly quickly, and will scamper among oriental hellebores (*Helleborus hybridus*), wild primroses, and wood anemones (*Anemone nemerosa*) with abandon.

In an already wooded garden where trees have built up a high canopy, there would be room to plant a few suitably drought-tolerant shrubs to create an intermediate layer. Spotted-leaved evergreen *Aucuba japonica*, spiny *Mahonia ×media* 'Charity', or perhaps neat evergreen Christmas box (*Sarcococca*), with its delicious winter perfume, are all adaptable and widely available. Then the drought-tolerant epimediums and their fellow bed-mates could snuggle in, around, and between the shrubs, creating a mature effect.

Many of the epimediums that tolerate dry shade have light yellow flowers that would blend in alongside the aucuba and the mahonia. Yellow is a good colour in deep shade, as it glows like a lantern. One of the most dramatic golden-leaved plants for dry shade is *Convallaria majalis* 'Golden Jubilee'. Like all lilies-of-the-valley it can cover the ground well and is very easy to propagate and increase.

Garden bluebells can be quite invasive in the border

> ### Spreading Epimediums
>
> *Epimedium* acuminatum
> *Epimedium* 'Amber Queen'
> *Epimedium davidii*
> *Epimedium* 'Domino'
> *Epimedium grandiflorum* 'Pink Parasol'
> *Epimedium ogisui*
> *Epimedium* ×*omeiense* 'Myriad Years'
> *Epimedium perralderianum*
> *Epimedium* 'Space Wagon'
> *Epimedium* 'Yōkihi'

Clumps of *Epimedium* ×*rubrum* caper about in the woodland garden at Holt Farm in Somerset, England.

Epimedium ×*versicolor* is an energetic spreader in the dry shade under a tree.

A ground-covering epimedium checks the spread of bluebells in a garden.

and difficult to eradicate once they have established themselves, but they also hold their own in the company of ground-covering epimediums. The bluebells spread quickly and would grow alongside the more generous forms of epimediums, battling it out in dry shade. In a wilder part of the garden they will make a classic perfumed sea of blue in late spring.

Both spreading wood spurge (*Euphorbia amygdaloides* var. *robbiae*) and the green-leaved form of Siberian bugloss (*Brunnera macrophylla*) can stand up to the bossier epimediums, as can lady's mantle (*Alchemilla mollis*) if it is allowed to self-seed. Dwarf comfrey (*Symphytum grandiflorum*) gently expands without much encouragement. All four of these woodland beauties would grow well and survive next to spreading epimediums in dry shade. Such foliage combinations would succeed where many plants require more moisture and light, and they could provide a sustainable, easily maintained planting scheme.

PLANTING SCHEMES FOR LESS-SPREADING, DROUGHT-TOLERANT SPECIES

Alpine epimedium (*Epimedium alpinum*), *E.* 'Asiatic Hybrid', *E.* 'Golden Eagle', *E.* ×*versicolor*, and *E.* ×*warleyense* are also comfortable in dry shade, and they cover the ground slightly less aggressively than *E.* ×*rubrum*. They enjoy good company. Classic Bowles' golden grass (*Milium effusum* 'Aureum'), whose leaves are the colour of butter, seeds around winningly, coming up in unexpected places. (But it betrays itself pretty quickly if it invades the space of something precious, so you can yank it out with a weeding fork.)

Welsh poppy (*Papaver cambricum*) also thrives in dry shade. The light yellow-flowered seedlings ally themselves well with *Epimedium* 'Golden Eagle', and *E.* ×*warleyense* would look lovely with the soft orange-flowered forms. Some scillas or squills are happy in dry shade under trees, and although they are not bossy plants, once they are at home, they will spread obligingly and light a bright blue candle at the same time as epimediums.

Brunnera macrophylla 'Jack Frost', a recent selection of Siberian bugloss, has white-veined leaves. It has smaller elbows than the type and puts up with the dry soils beneath trees. The leaves are as handsome as those of a hosta, but far less palatable to slugs and snails. The plant produces the typical bright blue forget-me-not flowers at the same time as epimediums. *Brunnera macrophylla* 'Mr Morse' has the same foliage but with white flowers. The leaves emerge small in spring during flowering but expand throughout the summer.

The small, creeping navelwort (*Omphalodes cappadocica*) weaves its way through a shady border and makes an easy friend to epimediums and their neighbours. The pretty blue flowers appear at the same time as epimediums, and the plant then makes a green carpet throughout the summer.

One or two geraniums tolerate very dry shade, although most prefer a somewhat more open position where they can enjoy the occasional rain shower. *Geranium macrorrhizum* 'Bevan's Variety' bears medium pink flowers in early summer and oddly scented leaves. The plant and its virginal sister, *G. macrorrhizum* 'White-Ness', which has not a hint of pink about her, make goodly mounds of foliage all summer, and steadily expand in the driest of shade.

Most gardeners are familiar with annual honesty (*Lunaria annua*) and are aware that it is perfectly at home in dry, shady soils, but perennial honesty (*L. rediviva*) is less familiar. It has similar seed pods, but they are oval rather than round. Its variegated form, *L. rediviva* 'Partway White', pushes up from the spring soil with a splash of mauve-pink about its white-and-green leaves. It beautifully accompanies epimediums as they start to extend their flowering stems, and by the time each has grown to maturity they settle down comfortably together in dry shade.

Clumping Epimediums

Epimedium 'Arctic Wings'
Epimedium 'Alabaster'
Epimedium acuminatum 'Galaxy'
Epimedium acuminatum 'Night Mistress'
Epimedium 'Artanis'
Epimedium brachyrrhizum
Epimedium 'Buckland Spider'
Epimedium 'Buff Beauty'
Epimedium 'Cyrion'
Epimedium grandiflorum 'Lilafee'
Epimedium grandiflorum 'Tama-no-genpei'
Epimedium 'Hina Matsuri'
Epimedium latisepalum
Epimedium ×*youngianum* 'Be My Valentine'
Epimedium ×*youngianum* 'Fairy Dust'

A mixed ground-cover of *Epimedium*, *Tiarella* (foamflower), and ferns.

For a pleasing combination in dry shade, try the semi-evergreen shield fern (*Polystichum setiferum*) with the evergreen *Epimedium* 'Amber Queen'.

Solomon's seal (*Polygonatum* ×*hybridum*) is another classic plant for dry shade that provides a vertical brush-stroke. Its elegant stems start to emerge in early spring and flower in late spring and early summer. Each flower is like an oval pearl droplet suspended from the arching stem. There are many different species and forms, all of which grow well in dry shade. Those with narrower leaves seem more resistant to sawfly. Possible choices could include *P. curvistylum*, with whorls of leaves and small mauve flowers, and even more diminutive *P. hookeri*, which makes dwarf mats of foliage and produces open mauve flowers in early summer.

Ferns thrive in shade, but only a few do well in drier soils in shade. Luckily, some of these are also semi-evergreen. Shield fern (*Polystichum setiferum*) and its varieties that are native to northern Europe, as well as North American *P. munitum*, grow well in such conditions. The latter eventually reaches heights of more than 1 m (40 in.), so it is definitely a background plant, or perhaps an evergreen companion to the magnificent spiny-leaved form of *Epimedium wushanense*.

Hart's tongue (*Asplenium scolopendrium*) is especially good in dry shade. Its crested forms (*A. scolopendrium* Cristatum Group) make wonderfully convoluted green mounds, like a mermaid's curly hair, and the cut-leaved form (*A. scolopendrium* 'Angustatum') is upright and erect in contrast to the horizontal foliage of epimediums. The particular light green of these ferns suits *Epimedium* flowers of any colour: it is the natural background to all our gardens in spring.

PLANTING SCHEMES FOR ACID SOILS

Most epimediums from Japan prefer acid soil with a pH below 6.5. Included here are certain species and the hybrids bred from them: *Epimedium sempervirens*; *E. grandiflorum*, its many named forms, and its hybrids *E.* ×*versicolor* and *E.* ×*youngianum*; and *E.* 'Akebono', which seems to be of the *E. grandiflorum* persuasion. If your garden soil has a low pH, you could grow most of the shade-loving plants detailed earlier, but there are some very beautiful plants that prosper only in acid shade. You cannot grow them anywhere else.

A few light trees, and one or two classic shrubs, can provide the right amount of shade for these denizens of acid soil.

Epimedium 'Akebono' prefers an acid soil.

Acid-loving Epimediums

Epimedium 'Akebono'
Epimedium 'Beni-kujaku' (probably)
Epimedium grandiflorum and selections
Epimedium 'Kodai Murasaki' (possibly)
Epimedium sempervirens and selections
Epimedium ×*youngianum* and selections

A woodland border at the Elisabeth C. Miller Botanical Garden in Seattle, Washington, features (from front to back) *Epimedium*, fragrant Solomon's seal (*Polygonatum odoratum*), and *Rhododendron*.

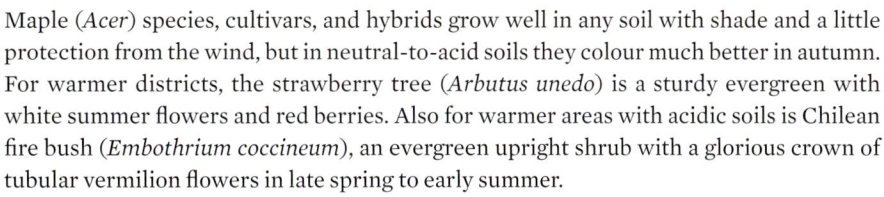

Maple (*Acer*) species, cultivars, and hybrids grow well in any soil with shade and a little protection from the wind, but in neutral-to-acid soils they colour much better in autumn. For warmer districts, the strawberry tree (*Arbutus unedo*) is a sturdy evergreen with white summer flowers and red berries. Also for warmer areas with acidic soils is Chilean fire bush (*Embothrium coccineum*), an evergreen upright shrub with a glorious crown of tubular vermilion flowers in late spring to early summer.

Most gardeners on acidic soils cannot resist one or two camellias to bring colour to their winter borders. These and witch hazel (*Hamamelis* ×*intermedia*) could play host to acid-loving epimediums. *Hamamelis* ×*intermedia* 'Pallida' is an exceptionally lovely selection with pale primrose yellow scented flowers in winter. Persian ironwood (*Parrotia persica*) is a relative of witch hazels whose glory lies in its autumn foliage, and sweetgum (*Liquidambar styraciflua*), a native of the eastern United States from Connecticut to Florida, has equally dramatic autumn foliage.

Rhododendrons are one of the most common shrubs planted on acidic soils. They contribute handsome evergreen foliage and flowers from early to late spring. The large-blooming hybrids so redolent of the early twentieth century seem to have fallen from favour lately, probably because they are deemed too big for today's small gardens. Some very special smaller-growing rhododendrons also make lower mounds of exceptionally beautiful foliage.

Azaleas and any of the dwarf forms, whether evergreen or deciduous, could form the backbone of a host of epimediums. Azaleas tend more towards yellows, oranges, and reds than their rhododendron sisters, although there are some very bright pinks among their number.

A high-profile plant that jumps out as ideal for acidic soil is the Himalayan blue poppy (*Meconopsis baileyi*). It is equally at home in neutral soil, but without acidity in the soil the flowers may be a wishy-washy mauve instead of that magical blue (or red, as in *M. punicea*). Himalayan blue poppy has a reputation for being difficult to grow, and it is even more challenging to propagate. It pays to select a plant with several side-shoots from the nursery. These smaller shoots will flower the following year.

In spring the many *Erythronium* species and cultivars, known more commonly as trout lilies or dog's tooth violets, seize attention for a few brief weeks. European species *E. dens-canis* and North American native *E. revolutum* produce pink flowers, while the hybrids 'Pagoda' and 'White Beauty' bear butter yellow and white flowers, respectively.

At Higher Cherubeer in Dolton, England, Jo and Tom Hynes maintain a large woodland garden on one acre in the rich acid soils of this farming county. When they moved to this part of Devon in the 1990s, Jo brought her collection of snowdrops and a few of the older varieties of ground-covering epimediums. Subsequently she met Julian Sutton of Desirable Plants in Devon, England, and was entranced by some of the new Chinese species and hybrid epimediums he offered. She purchased a few to plant in her woodland garden, which by then was maturing and shading the ground in summer, and yet full of empty pockets just right for another epimedium. In spring it is full of treasures, most of which would grow on any soil, not just acid loam. The garden is full of light trees, snaking paths winding their way through the woodland, and surprising corners. Although the garden is not self-consciously designed, Jo has an easy eye for colour. White, pale yellows, and lime green predominate in spring, and in a special corner Jo grows *Epimedium* 'King Prawn' where all her visitors can admire it.

Down in deepest Devon, England, north of the naval town of Plymouth, lies The Garden House at Buckland Monachorum, which has a good collection of epimediums growing in its acid soil. The Garden House has a long and involved history dating back centuries. It wound up in the care of Lionel and Katherine Fortescue, who started a successful commercial nursery on the site, growing large stock plants for the local wholesale

A path winds through the light woodland at Higher Cherubeer. Note the epimediums in the left foreground.

Epimedium 'King Prawn' is a special treasure in any garden.

nurseries. With his keen sense of colour and design, Lionel soon made the garden one of the most well known in the country. Before he and Katherine died in the early 1980s, they appointed Keith Wiley as head gardener, and under Wiley's supervision the cultivated area expanded into the surrounding six acres of paddocks outside the old walls. It has become one of the foremost gardens in the country for its cutting-edge planting design. Wiley was inspired by the natural flower-scapes of the world, such as those in South Africa, Colorado, and Crete. He did not seek to copy them, but to grasp the essence of each landscape. The result is innovative, filled with flowers, and unashamedly romantic. It speaks to every visitor.

The acid soil of The Garden House inspired Wiley to plant groves of azaleas and rhododendrons, camellias, magnolias, and eucryphias. Around the front lawn some of these provide a little shade for special woodland perennials: brunnera, lily-of-the-valley, trillium, corydalis. There are also much older plantings of the traditional ground-covering forms of *Epimedium* that romp away from the borders around the lawn, down the hill in the shade of the trees. In its role as a paradigm of innovative planting and plants, The Garden House has acquired a good collection of some of the most recently introduced epimediums.

Following Wiley's departure, the garden continues to exhibit cutting-edge plants and designs. Some of the new American hybrids bred by U.S. *Epimedium* hunter Darrell Probst have been planted in the acid soils of the borders around the front lawn, directly outside the house, in part sun. The mild, moist climate of Devon seems to temper the more open situation. Most of the plants have settled in well and are expanding. One or two seem to dislike the acidity, but time will tell.

PLANTING SCHEMES FOR CHINESE EPIMEDIUMS

Rarely in modern garden history has such a wealth of new plants suddenly become available to Western gardeners. The selection of epimediums can be overwhelming. Every plant contributes a unique combination of colour, height, and form, as well as character, beautiful foliage, and exquisite flowers.

The role of these new epimediums from China is far from the self-effacing background extras that gardeners have been growing for years. These are the divas. They should take centre stage in any spring planting, and their foliage has presence year-round.

Chinese epimediums need an improved soil rich in leaf mould, such as that found beneath trees, shrubs, roses, or conifers. The acidity or alkalinity of the soil is not as important, although shallow soils over chalk could present problems of lower fertility for some epimediums, and very acid soils are unsuitable for many. That said, Chinese epimediums are very easy to grow, and there are increasingly more of them available to European, American, and Australian gardeners. And there are other exceptional plants to grow over and around them. The effect can be like a treasure trove of precious stones.

Creating a canopy

If your garden lacks a shady spot for epimediums, planting birches is one of the fastest ways to create a woodland. Aside from the familiar stark white-barked silver birches (*Betula pendula* and relatives), you can find Chinese birches (*B. ermanii*) with coloured bark that varies from coral through mahogany-brown to purple-black. Each of the darker forms is beaded with white lenticels like pearls. An advantage of using birches to create shade is that they do not need to grow as a single, straight-stemmed trunk; they are available as multi-stemmed forms with three or four equally thick trunks arising from a single bole. In winter the colours are spectacular and echo many of the Chinese epimediums with coloured leaves. The multi-stemmed forms create light overhead shade quickly, within five to ten years, and would be a delight to plant beneath.

Flowering cherries are more short-lived than birches—25 years is a good age for a cherry—but planting pink- or white-flowered epimediums beneath would coincide with or quickly follow the showy blossoms, depending on spring

Multi-stemmed Himalayan birches (*Betula utilis* var. *jacquemontii*) under-planted with epimediums, ferns, and corydalis.

Epimediums in the light shade of *Magnolia sieboldii*.

conditions. Although birch bark cherry (*Prunus serrula*), also referred to as Tibetan cherry, is better known for its beautiful tan bark, and the winter-flowering cherry (*P. subhirtella* 'Autumnalis') starts flowering in late autumn and opens its buds a few at a time until early spring, they could play their roles well before the epimediums start to flower and would oversee the epimediums' glamorous winter foliage.

The closely related crab apples (*Malus* species) are well known for their flowers and autumn fruit, and rowan trees (*Sorbus*) could also audition for the role of fast-growing light woodland trees. If there is room for only a single tree to provide a bit of light shade, the weeping pear (*Pyrus salicifolia* var. *orientalis* 'Pendula') is a star—and one of the all-time favourites of Vita Sackville-West, who created Sissinghurst. This pear has pendulous branches with long silver leaves that emerge after the bright white flowers. These are followed in autumn by tiny pears like marzipan decorations. Even in winter the tree has an elegant umbrella shape—provided you regularly heighten the crown by pruning—with room underneath for any or many of the Chinese epimediums, especially those with pastel flowers.

Acer pensylvanicum flourishes with its head in the sun, making useful shadows beneath its branches. The serviceberrry *Amelanchier laevis* is a classic specimen tree that reaches about 5 m (17 ft.) after 10 years. It is widely grown for its bronze-pink young leaves that turn red in autumn, as well as its sprays of pure white flowers in late spring followed by red fruits. The Judas tree (*Cercis siliquastrum*) is another attractive spring performer. In mid-spring it bears clusters of bright pink flowers like small sweet peas, which mature to long purple pods in late summer, and its heart-shaped leaves appear at flowering time.

Katsura (*Cercidiphyllum japonicum*) is another slender tree that casts light shade. It has bronze new leaves in spring with inconspicuous flowers. However, in autumn it turns yellow, pink, and orange, and the dying leaves are famous for their aroma, which is redolent of burnt toffee.

Many magnolias flower a little later than the epimediums, and most grow better in a neutral-to-acid soil. However, the varieties of *Magnolia sieboldii* and *M. stellata* are much more tolerant of lime and would work well with the Chinese epimediums.

Diminutive *Hydrangea serrata* varieties are ideal shrubs to fill the shady border from mid-summer onwards. For the most part their flowers are subtle and quiet. Their petticoats could be formed of epimediums, ferns, and a host of other shade-lovers. There are numerous alternative species to the familiar mopheads and lacecaps of *H. macrophylla*. In particular, *H. involucrata* and its selections provide good company, and perhaps additional shade beneath the higher canopy, as would the creamy spikes of *H. paniculata*. *Hydrangea aspera* is big enough to provide its own micro-climate. This spectacular beauty is from the Himalayas, as befits such a large shrub. Its giant lace-cap flowers vary from the white *H. aspera* 'Peter Chappell' through the familiar lilac *H. aspera* 'Villosa' to the pink-flowered *H. aspera* 'Mauvette'.

Creating a lush ground layer
At a lower level, comprising the bottom storey of a shady garden, wild English primroses (*Primula vulgaris*) and wood anemones (*Anemone nemorosa*) provide a pleasant

accompaniment to flowering epimediums. Unfortunately, the visible presence of wood anemones in the garden is fleeting and confined to spring; the rest of the year is spent below ground, and it is all too frighteningly easy to put a trowel into a seemingly empty space and slice the little tubers into pieces. The wild form is simple, white, and beautiful, but there have been lots of selections, including double, crimped petalled flowers, and watery blue forms. A mixed group may interact and interbreed, and the results are lovely.

Corydalis flexuosa provides a great splash of true sky blue, that rare colour in the plant world. It is one of those plants that either grows for you to exhaustion or does not grow much at all. It seems to dislike damper soils and prefers, as do epimediums, a rich soil that also drains. At Wildside Nursery, Keith Wiley grows the brown-yellow *Epimedium* 'Honeybee' alongside this corydalis to great effect that riffs on the colours of the French Impressionists.

The natural habitat of most garden ferns is moist but draining shade, and there are one or two especially lovely forms of Japanese ferns that would unfurl their crosiers while the Chinese epimediums are flowering. Painted lady fern (*Athyrium niponicum* var. *pictum*) is silver-grey in its fronds with deep red veining, and eared lady fern (*A. otophorum* var. *okanum*) sports pale yellow fronds with pronounced red veins and stalks. Both dislike drafts, but once they are satisfied they grow away with aplomb.

The familiar old-fashioned columbines (*Aquilegia*) colonize shade very pleasantly. Their rosettes of leaves make good companions to flowering epimediums, and when these are all but faded, the columbines will open and take over.

Hardy geraniums hardly need an introduction. They usually flower after the epimediums have finished, and many spread—a lot. Plant them in the background, behind and away from the Chinese and Japanese epimediums, where they will fill in empty background spaces and produce clouds of flowers in mid-summer, some right up until the frosts. Some forms start and return to a small resting rosette without spreading outwards.

Plants with a trailing habit, such as *Geranium* 'Rozanne', *G.* 'Ann Folkard', or the similar but larger-flowered *G.* 'Sandrine', with brilliant magenta flowers and pronounced black eyes, could cover their neighbours from mid-summer onwards. Epimediums would probably not tolerate total submersion very well, so keep even these geraniums at a distance.

Lungworts (*Pulmonaria*) are an old cottage-garden favourite for growing in shade and between other plants, and do an excellent job of filling in awkward places. They

Overlapping seasons of bloom make *Epimedium acuminatum* 'Night Mistress' and a white-flowered bloodroot (*Sanguinaria*) ideal partners in a lush ground layer.

have been grown and selected for a long time, and there are some good new named forms available at garden centres and specialist nurseries. The rich velvet colours have been consolidated and improved, and the flower's wayward tendency to change colour has been diminished. Gardeners can also choose the hue of the leaves. In some varieties, the leaf spots have merged to form a solid silver-green that sets off the flowers.

Oriental hellebores have long been a gardener's favourite. Their lovely flowers open while the epimediums are still mounds of winter colour. They enjoy similar situations: hellebores take most of the moisture from the soil and allow the epimediums the good drainage they like.

Trilliums are native to the southeastern United States, where they grow in alkaline soil in woodland. For many years in Europe they had a reputation for being difficult to grow and for preferring acid soil. Neither is true. Today trilliums are propagated from

Epimedium brachyrrhizum and *Pulmonaria* 'Blue Ensign' in my garden.

Dark purple hellebores flower above epimediums before the latter get going.

seed rather than dug up, which risks tuber damage. The result is a plant that grows well and deeply, and specialist nursery owners and growers are loudly broadcasting the ability of these woodlanders to grow in alkaline soils (with a pH reading of 7.5 and above).

Deinanthe caerulea and its white sister *D. bifida* are closely related to hydrangeas but seldom seen in gardens, yet they are relatively easy herbaceous perennials to grow in shady woodland soil. They flower in mid-summer, after the epimediums are over. Like hydrangeas, *D. caerulea* tends to make blue flowers in acidic soil and pink-mauve ones in alkaline conditions, and *D. bifida* has ivory-white flowers. They are quite unlike hydrangeas to the inexpert eye. They are coy. Each blossom bows its head meekly, but you will be rewarded by putting a finger under its chin and lifting its face. Each male flower has five or six rounded open-faced petals surrounding a trembling centre of mauve-blue or white stamens. The plants reach about 30 cm (12 in.) in woodland soil and tend to be more blue in acidic conditions, but are perfectly suitable for growing in alkaline soils.

Roscoea purpurea 'Blackthorn Hybrid' pierces through a dense layer of *Epimedium* foliage.

In any border there is a danger of creating a continuum of mounding plants, each with its foliage or flowers, like hills receding in the distance. From a design point of view it is good to interrupt this effect by placing one or two upright plants, such as tall ferns, *Polygonatum*, or *Smilacina racemosa* (syn. *Maianthemum racemosum*) with its fluffy cream flowers on upright stems.

Uvularia grandiflora is a fleeting North American native plant that makes an elegant companion to flowering epimediums. It pushes up through the warming soil in spring and lights up a border with its butter yellow flowers. The flowers hang down like little unfolding umbrellas, but with a twist on each petal. The plant prefers moist but draining woodland soil and eventually reaches about 75 cm tall by 30 cm wide (30 × 12 in.). It then dies back completely until the following spring, so it is advisable to insert a label, pushed down into the soil, to prevent accidentally slicing it up in summer.

Roscoea species have sturdy upright stems to punctuate the mounds typical of many borders. These exotic-looking ginger relatives are much hardier than they look. Usually they follow the flowering of most epimediums, pushing up around their skirts.

Looking for all the world like a grass, exotically named *Ypsilandra thibetica* produces plumes of cream tassels in early spring, then tinges purple as the flowers mature to coincide with the early epimediums.

The pale flowers of *Ypsilandra thibetica* show up well against the reddish stems of epimediums. Note the spiny epimedium leaf in the left foreground.

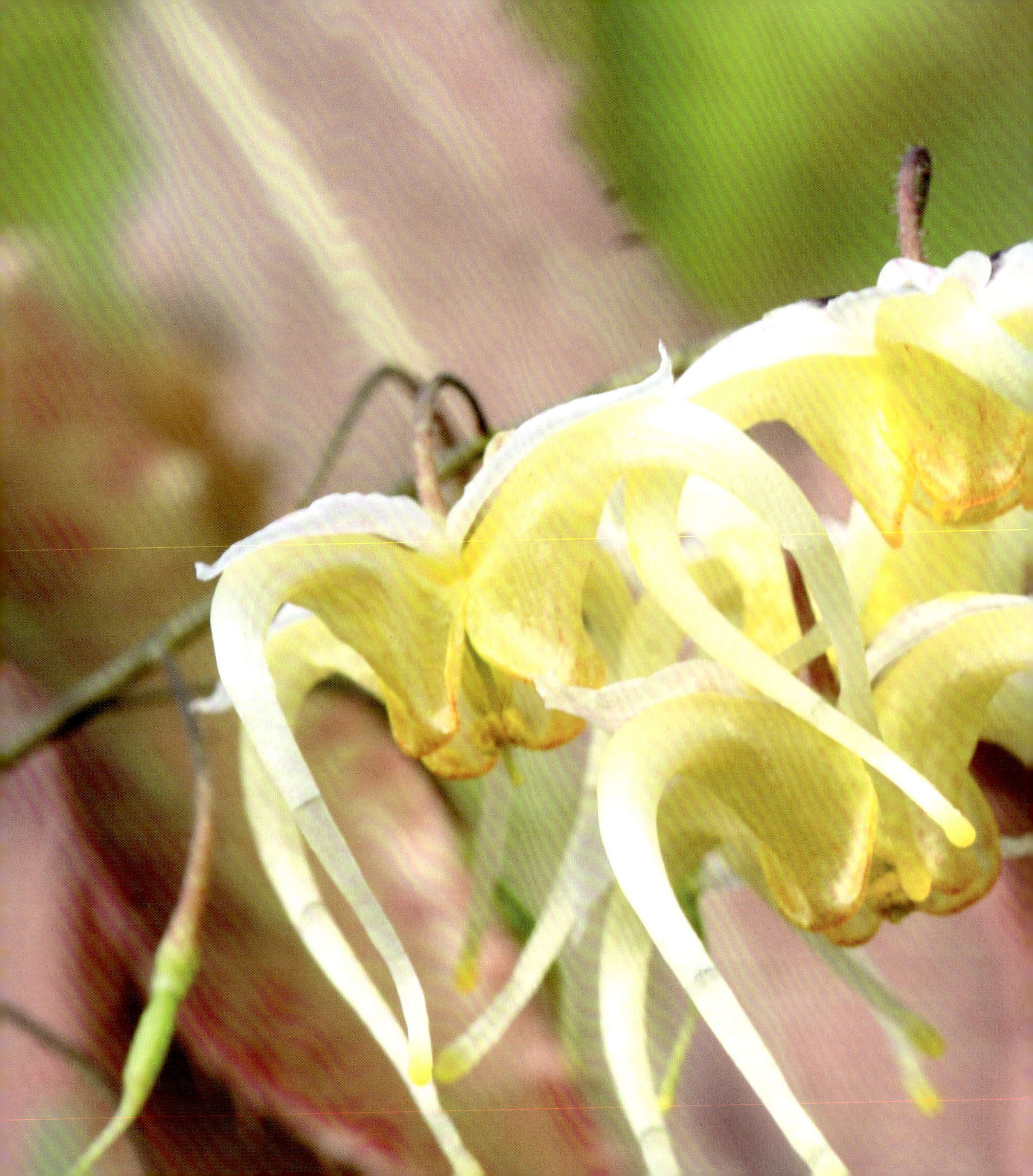

123 EPIMEDIUMS FOR THE GARDEN

Epimedium acuminatum

British plant-hunter Roy Lancaster collected this spectacular species around Emei Shan (Mount Omei) in Sichuan. He gathered it from around limestone cliffs in deciduous and coniferous woodland with moist soil. The clusters of up to 50 flowers have dark purple in-curved spurs and an open mouth beneath pale pink sepals. The young leaves are produced in threes and undulate along the edges. They are long and pointed and emerge mottled chestnut red, later maturing to green during the winter.

This species is variable in the wild, and it has crossed with *Epimedium fangii* to produce myriad coloured variants under the name *E.* ×*omeiense*, selected by Mikinori Ogisu and others. It has also been hybridized in cultivation with *E. dolichostemon* to produce *E.* 'Amanogawa' and *E.* 'Kaguyahime'.

ZONES 5–8
HEIGHT AND SPREAD 30 × 30–45 cm (12 × 12–18 in.)
FLOWERS spring

Epimedium acuminatum 'Galaxy'

This lovely plant is the result of Roy Lancaster's second collection of the species on Emei Shan (Mount Omei). He germinated just one seed from a single pod, which produced this quite different form. The clusters of large creamy white flowers dangle down on long, arching stems. The evergreen foliage renews itself in spring with warm red, pointed trifoliate leaves, which become more green and bristly when mature.

ZONES 5–8
HEIGHT AND SPREAD 30 × 30 cm (12 × 12 in.)
FLOWERS spring

Epimedium acuminatum 'Night Mistress'

Darrell Probst collected this plant from a remote spot near Nanchuan in Chongqing, Sichuan, and he considers it well worth the uncomfortable half-day drive along a winding road. 'Night Mistress' ticks all the boxes. It resembles the species in colouring, but with larger, more intensely hued flowers. The pale pink sepals contrast vividly with the deepest royal purple spurred petals, and there is a pleasing neatness about the flowers. They are more than 2 cm (1 in.) wide and open from spring into the summer. The flower stems arch over a 30- to 33-cm (12- to 15-in.) mound of long, tapering evergreen leaves with bristles around the margins. (Hence its specific name *acuminatum*, which means pointed.) The foliage is bronze in spring and gradually matures to green.

ZONES 5–8
HEIGHT AND SPREAD 30–38 × 30 cm (12–15 × 12 in.)
FLOWERS spring and into early summer

51

Epimedium 'Akebono'

SYNONYM *Epimedium* 'Dawn'

The precise parentage of this Japanese plant is not known, although it seems to be of the *Epimedium ×youngianum* persuasion with deciduous foliage. The sepals are white and palest pink resting atop long spurred petals that are deeper rose pink in the centre, edged with crystal white around the mouth and at the tip of the long spurs. Its clumps increase in size year after year. It prefers an acid soil.

ZONES 4–9
HEIGHT AND SPREAD 18 × 30 cm (7 × 12 in.)
FLOWERS early to late spring

Epimedium 'Alabaster'

SYNONYM *Epimedium* 'Conalba'

American enthusiast Richard Lighty discovered this plant in his garden in Pennsylvania. He believes it is a seedling of *Epimedium diphyllum* crossed with a white *E.* ×*youngianum*, but it does not appear to be an acid-loving specimen. The outer sepals are small and dark rose pink, echoing the colour of the thin stems, and the petals are pure white and spurless, like a white form of *E.* ×*youngianum* 'Merlin'. It is herbaceous, with spring green young foliage that sets off the flowers, making a low mound of triangular leaves that lights up the shade garden. It is easy to grow in almost any soil that is not boggy. Propagation for re-sale is prohibited.

ZONES 4–8
HEIGHT AND SPREAD 18 × 20 cm (7 × 8 in.), eventually
FLOWERS mid-spring

Epimedium 'Amanogawa'

SYNONYM *Epimedium* 'Milky Way'

This plant is another good Japanese *Epimedium acuminatum* hybrid, crossed with *E. dolichostemon* to produce clouds of flowers with big white sepals over smaller purple-brown petals whose tips are primrose yellow. The appearance is delicate, seemingly ephemeral, and distinctly spring-like. The flowers are held well above the red-splashed young leaves, like butterflies alighting on the wiry stems. Thereafter the leaves are evergreen and contribute a useful presence in the winter garden.

ZONES 5–8
HEIGHT AND SPREAD 30 × 30 cm (12 × 12 in.)
FLOWERS spring

Epimedium 'Amber Queen'

Robin White, of the former Blackthorn Nursery in Hampshire, England, made this easily available hybrid from a selection of seedlings of *Epimedium wushanense* 'Caramel' and *E. flavum*. It has proved to be an excellent garden plant and makes its presence felt in many shady borders. It creates a large evergreen clump of dramatic leaves, and the flowers open as an abundance of very tall marmalade orange blooms. Closer examination reveals a subtle variation of colour. The small, rounded pale orange sepals protect big spurred petals that are pale creamy white with a dark orange mouth and light yellow tips to the white spurs. The plant flowers over a long period, often repeating in early autumn, making it one of the longest-performing epimediums in the garden. The new foliage is mottled with splashes of burgundy-red and matures to make long, very pointed green leaves that make quite an impact all through the year. Propagation for re-sale is prohibited.

ZONES 5–8
HEIGHT AND SPREAD 30 × 45 cm (12 × 18 in.)
FLOWERS spring, sometimes repeats in early autumn

Epimedium 'Ambrosine'

Renowned French *Epimedium* breeder Thierry Delabroye has selected this beautiful hybrid, named for his daughter, with palest peach-pink sepals and spurs held horizontally over a darker apricot centre, opening from darker buds. The foliage is fresh green speckled with apricot.

ZONES 5–8
HEIGHT AND SPREAD 30 × 30 cm (12 × 12 in.)
FLOWERS spring

Epimedium 'Arctic Wings'

Robin White created this newer hybrid by crossing *Epimedium latisepalum* and *E. ogisui*. Both sepals and spurred petals are large and white. The flowers are similar to *E. ogisui*, but twice the size and a cleaner, brighter white. They are enhanced by the sharp lemon yellow stamens and pale apple green stems. This plant forms a good-size clump of evergreen crinkled leaves with spiny edges. The foliage emerges in spring well splashed with bronze. Propagation for re-sale is prohibited.

ZONES 6–9
HEIGHT AND SPREAD 30 × 18 cm (12 × 7 in.)
FLOWERS spring

Epimedium 'Artanis'

Thierry Delabroye bred this striking plant, which has big evergreen leaves mottled with oxblood red splashes. In spring, a large flower emerges from slightly grey-purple outer sepals. The inner sepals are light rose red over wide-open spurs. These have light yellow tips that gradually shade to rich cranberry red. The centre of the flower is deep red-purple. The flowers arch well above the foliage on long 30- to 45-cm (12- to 18-in.) stalks.

ZONES 4–8
HEIGHT AND SPREAD 30 × 30 cm (12 × 12 in.) at present
FLOWERS spring

Epimedium 'Black Sea'

This is the plant to grow for winter colour. Its unusual form glories in its deep red foliage, which is produced as autumn temperatures drop and frosts arrive. In some years the leaves turn the eponymous black and shiny. They last throughout winter and into early spring, when it is advisable to cut them back before the early flowers arise. However, in a particularly cold spring it would be worth waiting until the worst of the frosts are over. The flowers are quite small but grow in a profusion of almost translucent light orange and primrose yellow, and they dance over the leaves on wiry red stems that add to their charm. 'Black Sea' was thought to be a cultivar of the ground-covering *Epimedium pinnatum* subsp. *colchicum*, but has proved to be a hybrid. It does not tolerate dry shade like its hypothetical parent, but its good winter presence and the fact that it flowers very early in a mild spring make it an exceptional addition to a shady spot.

ZONES 5–9
HEIGHT AND SPREAD 30 × 60 cm (12 × 24 in.) after a couple of years in the right conditions
FLOWERS early to mid-spring, depending on the warmth of the season

Epimedium brachyrrhizum

Visually this species is very similar to *Epimedium leptorrhizum*, differing botanically only in the size and thickness of its rhizomes and the length of its stems (the latter is shorter, about 15 cm [6 in.]). One of the easily identifiable differences is the number of hairs on the leaves: *E. brachyrrhizum* has 17 to 20 spines per 5 cm (2 in.) of leaf margin, whereas *E. leptorrhizum* has 10 to 13. This makes it easier to separate them than measuring the length of the stems and rhizomes. However, the thicker, shorter rhizomes mean that it spreads more slowly than *E. leptorrhizum*.

The plant bears some of the largest flowers in the genus: about 4 cm (1.5 in.) across on a well-grown specimen. The sepals are long and wide enough to cover the petals. In the most commonly grown clone, they are a uniform pale rose pink above in-curved spurred petals that are a slightly darker pink at the mouth and translucent white at the tips. The effect is of a nest of pink spiders poised on 30-cm (12-in.) light brown stalks. The leathery evergreen leaves are held in threes on the flowering stalk and turn red, cranberry, and deep green in winter. In spring, the plants renew themselves with red mottled foliage. The wild species is notably variable in leaf and flower colour, from lavender-pink to white to deep lavender.

There are one or two U.S. selections of *Epimedium brachyrrhizum*, notably *E. brachyrrhizum* 'Karen' (see the next entry).

ZONES 5–8
HEIGHT AND SPREAD 35 × 25–30 cm (14 × 10–12 in.)
FLOWERS early spring

Epimedium brachyrrhizum 'Karen'

Darrell Probst selected this seedling in 2000 and named it after Karen Perkins. It is a prolific, exceptionally large-flowered form. The young evergreen leaves emerge a deep cranberry rose in spring among the mature green. They set off the flowers well.

ZONES 5–8
HEIGHT AND SPREAD 18 × 30 cm (7 × 12 in.)
FLOWERS spring

Epimedium brevicornu

This charming, dainty species was collected by Mikinori Ogisu in Sichuan. It is one of the first to flower in spring, with a constellation of tiny white stars with bright yellow anthers and stamens that seem to twinkle above the light green leaves. Legendary plant-collector Reginald Farrer first described it at the turn of the twentieth century. Closer examination reveals small dark outer sepals over large white inner sepals. The petals are small, with just the merest hint of a spur and with yellow margins around the mouth that echo the stamens. The young, papery leaves are deciduous, heart-shaped, and light green, deepening in colour as they mature.

ZONES 4–8 (Karen Perkins considers it to be very cold hardy, maybe to Zone 3, but it may not do so well in warmer climates)
HEIGHT AND SPREAD 30–40 × 30 cm (12–16 × 12 in.)
FLOWERS spring
RELATED PLANTS
Epimedium brevicornu var. *rotundatum* is supposedly a smaller form of the species, but William Stearn seems not to have encountered or recognized it. Darrell Probst also collected the plant, and Garden Vision Epimediums has many different clones of it for sale that vary widely in leaf size and colour in spring. Their height can range from 20 to 35 cm (8–14 in.).

Epimedium 'Buckland Spider'

Keith Wiley bred this striking cultivar at Wildside Nursery in Devon, England, by crossing *Epimedium grandiflorum* with *E. koreanum* to produce dusky pink flowers. The sepals are slightly mottled and streaked pink, and they nearly cover the pale pink petals. Those pictured are icy pink with white-tipped spurs up to 4 cm (1.5 in.) across. Like its Japanese parent, the plant has deciduous foliage that re-emerges in spring bronze-red and slowly fades to provide a bright apple green background. It is proving to be tolerant of alkaline soils.

ZONES 5–8
HEIGHT AND SPREAD 30 × 30 cm (12 × 12 in.) and beyond
FLOWERS spring

Epimedium 'Buff Beauty'

Keith Wiley also produced this second new hybrid. Its deep purple stems and outer sepals highlight the open white and pale lemon yellow flowers held well above the foliage. The inner sepals are white, fading to palest rose pink in the centre, over long white up-tilted spurs just tipped with lemon yellow. The middle of the flower is edged with pale yellow that fades back to the centre. The evergreen leaves are slightly tinged copper when young, and the whole plant makes a subtle addition to the shade garden.

ZONES 5–8, probably
HEIGHT AND SPREAD 30 × 30 cm (12 × 12 in.) until proven otherwise
FLOWERS spring

Epimedium campanulatum

This dainty little species has clouds of small flowers in a vibrant yellow that resemble the eponymous bell flowers in shape. Beneath its red-tinged sepals, its simple petals are rounded and in-curved. They have no spurs, like *Epimedium platypetalum* and *E. ecalcaratum*, but their flowers have a more box-like formation. The leaves are evergreen and heart-shaped; they emerge a light apple green in spring and set off the flowers well. Although it does not grow strongly, with a little care and allowed its own space it makes a delicate addition to a shady border. Mikinori Ogisu discovered the plant in Dujiangyan, Sichuan, in 1994, and brought it to the United Kingdom.

ZONES 5–8
HEIGHT AND SPREAD 30 × 30 cm (12 × 12 in.)
FLOWERS spring

Epimedium 'Candy Striper'

This startlingly different hybrid is unique. It bears clusters of small flowers with a white background and a distinctive rose pink stripe down the middle of each petal. The petals are held apart from each other to give the flowers wide-open faces. The foliage is herbaceous, the leaves emerging green with a slight purple margin to set off the flowers.

ZONES 5–8
HEIGHT AND SPREAD 38–40 × 30 cm (15–16 × 12 in.)
FLOWERS mid-spring

Epimedium chlorandrum

This species, which Mikinori Ogisu collected in Sichuan, has large flowers with slightly upturned outer sepals like the roofs of Chinese pagodas. The sepals and the open-spurred petals are primrose yellow with darker yellow tips to the spurs. The plant's name derives from the Greek for a green flower and refers to the stamens and anthers, a feature it shares with only *Epimedium pubescens* and *E. fargesii*. The flowers soar above the new horizontal leaves, which are large and splashed red-brown with pronounced spines.

ZONES 5–8
HEIGHT AND SPREAD 35–65 × 30 cm (14–26 × 12 in.)
FLOWERS early spring

Epimedium 'Chocolatte'

In this plant, Tony Avent has selected a chocoholic's dream. The flowers are shades of light brown with white inner sepals over in-curved pale beige petals with a milk chocolate mouth highlighted brown. The flowers nestle above and among dark brown young leaves. The foliage is semi-evergreen and vigorous. The plant is delicious and definitely not fattening!

ZONES 5–8
HEIGHT AND SPREAD 50 × 30 cm (20 × 12 in.)
FLOWERS spring

Epimedium 'Cyrion'

Thierry Delabroye raised this hybrid, which has especially well-marked and mottled leaves that are brown-red on green. The flowers are spectacular, with rich red-pink sepals over darkest purple-centred petals that extend to translucent white spurs. The prominent yellow stamens light up the whole plant.

ZONES 4–8
HEIGHT AND SPREAD 30 × 30 cm (12 × 12 in.) at present
FLOWERS spring

Epimedium davidii

Plant-hunter Armand David first collected this species in the late nineteenth century from Baoxing, Sichuan. (David, a missionary priest to China, is famous for "discovering" the giant panda, among other things.) The plant has cheerful buttercup yellow petals with long upturned spurs beneath russet brown sepals. The stems, which are an attractive dark coral-red, hold the flowers above the evergreen foliage, which opens similarly bronzed and matures to shining green with seemingly prickly leaves. It makes a vigorous clump without running in European gardens, but in the United States it is found to be less easy.

ZONES 5–8
HEIGHT AND SPREAD 30 × 45 cm (12 × 18 in.)
FLOWERS late spring and sporadically throughout the summer

Epimedium dolichostemon

This plant was the first of the many new species from China that Mikinori Ogisu introduced. He collected it in 1988 under the name *Epimedium fargesii*, which it strongly resembles. William Stearn later identified it as a separate species. The small white-and-mauve flowers of this species are borne generously. They have bright white rounded sepals held horizontally over small bronze-purple in-curved petals. The long protruding stamens with yellow-green filaments give the multitude of flowers the appearance of a flight of small hummingbirds. The evergreen leaves are long, pointed, and splashed light bronze in spring.

ZONES 5–8
HEIGHT AND SPREAD 30 × 30 cm (12 × 12 in.)
FLOWERS spring

Epimedium 'Domaine de St Jean de Beauregard'

Thierry Delabroye bred this enchanting new epimedium, which is included in his top 10 new hybrids. He picked it out for its tall flower spike held well above the leaves, which are lightly speckled with red-bronze when young. The flowers are a complex mixture. The sepals are red in the centre, edged in translucent white, and flick up as the flower opens. The petals that emerge are like spiders in party dresses. They have wide pale cream spurs that end in little yellow spots, and then darken through light yellow to red-orange in the centre.

ZONES 5–8
HEIGHT AND SPREAD 70–80 × 60 cm (28–32 × 24 in.)
FLOWERS spring

Epimedium 'Domino'

Darrell Probst bred and introduced this especially lovely hybrid in 2004. Its sprays of large flowers are held 60 cm (24 in.) above mounds of long spiny leaves that are splashed with bronze. The flowers are numerous and crowded, with sepals and long-spurred white petals deepening to a contrasting purple-red centre. The effect is very striking. This plant is sure to win lots of friends in Europe, as it has done in the United States, especially because it produces a second flush of flowers if planted in the right position.

ZONES 5–8
HEIGHT AND SPREAD 60 × 100 cm (24 × 40 in.)
FLOWERS spring

Epimedium ecalcaratum

In this Chinese species, the brightness of colour compensates for the small size of the flowers. Mikinori Ogisu collected it from Baoxing, Sichuan. He noted that in the wild, the simple bell-shaped flowers begin to form spurs in the corners like a box. In the garden, the butter yellow bells are suspended over the re-emerging green and light bronze leaves to form a neat clump. The sepals are small and bronze-red, as are the thin stems that hold the sprays of flower aloft above the foliage.

ZONES 5–8
HEIGHT AND SPREAD 25–30 × 30 cm (10–12 × 12 in.)
FLOWERS spring

Epimedium 'Egret'

This lovely epimedium is another new form from Thierry Delabroye. It is the result of hybridizing *Epimedium franchetii* and *E. latisepalum* to produce large flowers that are held clear of the coloured spring leaves. The large cream sepals are held up above the longer spurred lemon yellow petals. It is a fresh, clean combination. The evergreen foliage re-emerges in spring with soft brown-red marbling, and the whole becomes a beautiful foliage plant.

ZONES 5–8
HEIGHT AND SPREAD 30 × 30 cm (12 × 12 in.)
FLOWERS spring

Epimedium 'Enchantress'

Elizabeth Strangman, of the former Washfield Nursery in Kent, England, discovered this cross between *Epimedium dolichostemon* and *E. leptorrhizum* in the mid-1990s. It has become a classic hybrid. It bears medium-size flowers similar to *E. dolichostemon*, but on longer flower stalks. The grey-lavender sepals and petals do not have a well-defined spur. The central eye of the petals is stained indigo-purple, from which protrudes prominent yellow stamens like its parent. The flowers are held above evergreen foliage that is marbled and splashed dark red when it renews itself in spring. The foliage colours well in autumn—especially in the United States, according to Karen Perkins—and spreads on long, thin 15-cm (6-in.) rhizomes.

ZONES 5–8
HEIGHT AND SPREAD 15–20 × 30 cm (6–8 × 12 in.)
FLOWERS spring

Epimedium epsteinii
Epstein's epimedium

This striking epimedium was named in honour of the late Harold Epstein of New York, who was a renowned grower of epimediums and President Emeritus of the North American Rock Garden Society. The Beijing Botanic Garden in Hunan collected the plant in 1994, and Darrell Probst distributed it.

The deep purple-red spurred petals extend past the circlet of wide white sepals to remarkable effect. The spurs pale a little towards the darker tips, and the centre of the sepals is slightly tinged light purple. The effect is one of startling contrast. The slightly toothed evergreen leaves re-emerge with a light bronze cast to mature deep glossy green. The drama of its colouring makes up for its slight reluctance to flower.

The plant generally grows well in a leafy, humus-rich soil in light shade. However, Karen Perkins finds it difficult. She suggests it may be at the top range of hardiness in the United States, or that it might dislike acid soils. It spreads with long, thin 15- to 20-cm (6- to 8-in.) rhizomes.

ZONES 5–8, probably
HEIGHT AND SPREAD 25 × 30 cm (10 × 12 in.)
FLOWERS spring

Epimedium fangii

This species, which was found growing on Emei Shan (Mount Omei), is the parent of a number of naturally occurring hybrids that Mikinori Ogisu discovered. It is evergreen, with newly emergent near-black leaves on dark stems that set off the uniformly bright yellow spurred flowers. These blooms open from beneath small sepals that are white with a frilled raspberry pink edge. The petals around the mouth are slightly pointed, giving it a distinct appearance. It spreads energetically without becoming invasive.

ZONES 5–8
HEIGHT AND SPREAD 30 × 60 cm (12 × 24 in.)
FLOWERS spring

Epimedium fargesii
Farges' epimedium

Paul Farges collected this species, which is very similar to *Epimedium dolichostemon*, in Sichuan in 1894. However, it has proved to be a variable species in the wild, and when Mikinori Ogisu collected it again, he noticed that the plant differed slightly from *E. dolichostemon* both botanically and in its colouring. It was recognized as true *E. fargesii* from the original dried specimens, and this is the plant that is distributed today.

It has clouds of small flowers with straight lavender to white sepals that gradually reflex back as they fully open to resemble the feathers on a shuttlecock. The short, slightly spurred petals are deep purple, and the shape of the flower accentuates the prominent green anthers and stamens that point down like a bird's beak. The young leaves re-emerge in spring with red veining and a distinct red cast. The foliage then matures to medium green, and sometimes the spring markings re-emerge as purple-black blotches at the onset of cold weather. According to Karen Perkins' observations in the United States, its clumps are among the most vigorous of the Chinese species.

ZONES 5–8
HEIGHT AND SPREAD 25 cm (10 in.) in flower by about 30 cm (12 in.) across after a couple of years
FLOWERS from early to late spring, according to climate and weather

Epimedium fargesii 'Pink Constellation'

This is a lovely selection of a pretty species. It differs from the species in the pinker colouring of its sepals and deeper, more precisely coloured purple-centred petals.

ZONES 5–8
HEIGHT AND SPREAD 45 × 30 cm (18 × 12 in.)
FLOWERS from early to late spring, according to the climate and weather

Epimedium 'Fire Dragon'

This excellent hybrid from Robin White crosses *Epimedium davidii* with *E. leptorrhizum*. It is a striking, startling combination of salmon pink sepals held above long, in-curved white spurred petals melting into primrose yellow centres with prominent yellow stamens. The flowers are held on dark purple stems well above the strong green foliage. The light brown young leaves provide a contrasting background. The plant flowers until early summer, and the handsome clumps of light green foliage remain all winter. Propagation for re-sale is prohibited.

ZONES 5–8
HEIGHT AND SPREAD 18–50 × 30 cm (7–20 × 12 in.)
FLOWERS early spring into summer

Epimedium 'Flowers of Sulphur'

Robin White created this hybrid by crossing *Epimedium flavum* and *E. ogisui*. Curiously, the plant is herbaceous despite its evergreen parents. It bears clusters of tall spikes of primrose yellow flowers with dusky red outer sepals. The paler inner sepals overlie yellow-tipped spurred petals that resolve into sulphur bells with a light yellow margin. The foliage emerges red-bronze with green veins to set off the flowers beautifully. It matures to apple green. Propagation for re-sale is prohibited.

ZONES 5–6
HEIGHT AND SPREAD 35 × 40 cm (14 × 16 in.)
FLOWERS spring

Epimedium franchetii 'Brimstone Butterfly'

Mikinori Ogisu introduced *Epimedium franchetii* from Hubei in the mid-1980s under the name *E. hunanense*, but this cultivar, which William Stearn named in 1996, is commonly grown. Although there is some doubt about whether it is a selection of *E. franchetii* or if there is another species in its parentage, most experts agree that it is a hybrid. The truth is academic, but the reality is a remarkably beautiful plant. It bears large two-tone soft yellow flowers with palest primrose sepals that curve over the centre of sulphur yellow long-spurred petals with yellow tips. The blossoms are held suspended above the young evergreen foliage, which emerges deep salmon pink and ages to make large, leathery green leaves.

ZONES 5–8
HEIGHT AND SPREAD 45–60 × 30 cm (18–24 × 12 in.)
FLOWERS early spring into summer

Epimedium 'Fukujuji'

This relatively new introduction from Japan resembles *Epimedium grandiflorum* in many ways. However, it is semi-evergreen and loses its leaves only in a severe winter. It has relatively large deep rose pink flowers that are shaggy and delicate. The blooms are followed by fresh new leaves on thin wiry stems.

ZONES 5–8
HEIGHT AND SPREAD 25 × 30 cm (10 × 12 in.) in flower
FLOWERS spring

Epimedium grandiflorum
Large-flowered barrenwort

Philipp Franz von Siebold introduced this clump-forming species from Japan in 1830. The Japanese name, *Ikariso*, refers to a flower in the form of an anchor with a claw on each corner, which was traditionally used by Japanese fishermen.

In the first half of the nineteenth century, very few *Epimedium* species were known in Europe. Von Siebold planted those that survived a six-month voyage from Japan in the Ghent University Botanic Garden in Belgium, and they caused quite a stir. The plants grew well in the garden's rich, shady acid soil, and were propagated and distributed throughout Europe.

Since then this species has been crossed and selected to provide gardeners with some excellent named forms. The flowers of von Siebold's original plants were white and pale purple, but this is a very variable species that has produced some remarkable cultivars with widely different coloured flowers ranging from white through pinks and lilacs, to red-purple. Some have striking dark red-black leaf margins, or even entirely purple leaves. And many varieties exhibit a second growth flush later in the summer. The photo shows a pink form.

As with so many Japanese plants, *Epimedium grandiflorum* prefers acid conditions and the usual fertile leafy soil in light shade. If you top-dress the plant with leaf mould in early spring, it will repay you by growing steadily and well. It is herbaceous but the foliage provides displays of reds, oranges, and yellows in autumn before dying down for the winter. If it is necessary to water, the ideal choice is acid water (such as rainwater). The plant can absorb iron through the addition of a sequestrate.

The varieties described are merely a selection of what is available in European and American nurseries. The list is growing constantly. Hardiness, size, and season of bloom all depend on the particular cultivar.

ZONES 4–9
HEIGHT AND SPREAD up to 60 × 45 cm (24 × 18 in.)
FLOWERS spring

Epimedium grandiflorum 'Akagiza Kura'

The name of this Japanese cultivar seems to have been split up oddly. Originally it may have been 'Akagi Zakura', which means red cherry. However, the plant is not red, but a unique shade of pastel apricot. The flowers emerge against light green leaves to produce a very feminine plant. They open from apple green outer sepals on long similarly coloured stalks. The large inner sepals are held over the taloned petals which deepen to a rosier pink-apricot at the centre. The plant spreads slowly.

ZONES 4–8
HEIGHT AND SPREAD 35 cm (14 in.), eventually
FLOWERS spring

Epimedium grandiflorum 'Beni Chidori'

The name of this Japanese variety means red plover. Its inner sepals are held horizontally and detached above the petals in a rich shade of magenta. The petals have open white-tipped spurs that become a deep carmine-purple at the mouth of the flowers, which are held above the emerging foliage on long black stems. The leaves are fresh green, with the trace of a dark margin when young.

ZONES 4–9
HEIGHT AND SPREAD 15–40 × 30 cm (6–16 × 12 in.)
FLOWERS spring

Epimedium grandiflorum 'Circe'

This form, which Darrell Probst introduced in 2006, is becoming increasingly available. It has clouds of deeper, more evenly carmine-purple flowers than *Epimedium grandiflorum* 'Beni Chidori'. The sepals stand clear above the long-spurred petals, which bear crisp white tips. They deepen to purple at the centre and are held aloft above the dusky purple young leaves on red stems. The foliage turns medium green in summer. 'Circe' is closer in appearance to *E. grandiflorum* 'Yubae', but is shorter and has more flowers.

ZONES 4–9
HEIGHT AND SPREAD 28 × 30 cm (11 × 12 in.)
FLOWERS spring

Epimedium grandiflorum 'Dark Beauty'

Although this cultivar is not yet available in Europe, it is a fine plant that will doubtless make its way across the pond. It appeared in the garden of the late Harold Epstein, who thought it was the result of a cross between *Epimedium grandiflorum* 'Yubae' and *E.* 'Silver Queen'. The plant has especially dark brown-purple new foliage that emerges early in spring with large rose pink flowers. The dark pink inner sepals are held above paler flowers whose long spurs are white suffused rose. It often produces a second flush of flowers later in spring. This plant spreads slowly, reaching 30 cm (12 in.) after a year or two.

ZONES 4–9
HEIGHT AND SPREAD 20 × 30 cm (8 × 12 in.)
FLOWERS spring, and repeats later

Epimedium grandiflorum var. higoense 'Bandit'

Darrell Probst introduced this remarkable selection from Japan into the West on more than one occasion. The plant he originally bought at We Du Nursery differed markedly from that of the same name he purchased 11 years later. Probst trialled them for many years and eventually selected this form for its pink-bronze young leaves that emerge before the flowers and develop a deep purple-black margin to each leaf. The entirely white flowers are suspended above the foliage on long dark purple stems, and the plant grows a second flush of leaves that eventually reach 30 cm (12 in.). When flowering, the plant is small and low growing, but very eyecatching at the front of a shady border.

ZONES 4–8
HEIGHT AND SPREAD 15–30 × 30 cm (6–12 × 12 in.)
FLOWERS spring, and repeats later

Epimedium grandiflorum var. *higoense* 'Confetti'

Like dancing flakes of spring snow, the flowers are entirely white on pale beige stems, and each leaf has different light purple speckles and splashes, which gives the whole plant a frothy air. Gradually the foliage resolves into green to make an attractive fine-textured mound throughout the summer. Darrell Probst introduced and bred it in 2007. The plant produces a taller flush of second growth up to 25–30 cm (10–12 in.).

ZONES 4–8
HEIGHT AND SPREAD 18 × 30 cm (7 × 12 in.)
FLOWERS spring, and repeats later

Epimedium grandiflorum var. higoense 'Saturn'

This lovely plant has pure white flowers that open from dusky purple buds and outer sepals. The young leaves have margins in deep brown-maroon that resemble the eponymous planet's rings. American *Epimedium* enthusiast Dick Weaver named the plant, which was introduced from China in 1991. It produces a taller flush of second growth up to 20–25 cm (8–10 in.).

ZONES 4–8
HEIGHT AND SPREAD 10–13 × 30 cm (4–5 × 12 in.)
FLOWERS spring, and repeats later

Epimedium grandiflorum 'Koji'

The light purple-pink sepals sit slightly lifted atop the spurred petals. The spurs are white tipped merging to the same pale pink-purple that deepens towards the middle. The mouths have white margins. Flowers completely cover the plant in clusters about 20 cm (8 in.) tall on pale apple green stems. This form makes a good low-growing clump in light shade. In the United States, Garden Vision Epimediums lists this variety as a form of *Epimedium sempervirens*.

ZONES 4–8
HEIGHT AND SPREAD 20 × 30 cm (8 × 12 in.)
FLOWERS spring

Epimedium grandiflorum 'Korin'

This beautiful selection from Koen Van Poucke has very dark red flowers and even darker stems that stand out well against the fresh green leaves. Each leaf is faintly margined with dark red that resembles a stencil. The whole plant is visually striking.

ZONES 4–8
HEIGHT AND SPREAD 20–30 × 30 cm (8–12 × 12 in.)
FLOWERS spring

Epimedium grandiflorum 'La Rocaille'

This selection bears subtle flowers with white inner sepals shaded with lime green at the centre and small dusky purple outer sepals that give the flowers some zing. They are borne on distinctive light brown stems that provide additional impact. The spurred petals are creamy white with lime shading and narrow white margins around the mouth and at the tips of their spurs. The new leaves are large with fine teeth, and they have a light rose-purple blush that gradually becomes medium green in summer. This plant definitely bears closer examination.

ZONES 4–9
HEIGHT AND SPREAD 35 × 40–45 cm (14 × 16–18 in.)
FLOWERS spring

Epimedium grandiflorum 'Lilafee'

'Lilafee' (lilac fairy) is an old selection created by Ernst Pagels. It has tall grey-pink flowers on long purple stems that open from deeper purple buds. The paler mauve sepals are held upwards over light purple petals with long white spurs that are carried horizontally above the re-emerging foliage. The leaves are bronze purple when young, gradually aging to medium green as they mature.

ZONES 4–9
HEIGHT AND SPREAD 20 × 20 cm (8 × 8 in.)
FLOWERS spring

Epimedium grandiflorum 'Pink Parasol'

Tony Avent made this outstanding selection in 2005. It produces large rose pink flowers on tall red stalks over the young bronze clumps of leaves. The inner sepals are deep rose pink streaked with white, held above and away from the long white-tipped spurs. The mouth is also margined white. The plant is one of the most vigorous of its group.

ZONES 4–8
HEIGHT AND SPREAD 56 cm (22 in.) in flower, up to 75 cm (30 in.) across
FLOWERS early to late spring

Epimedium grandiflorum 'Purple Prince'

The sepals of this exceptionally purple form are inky purple-black when they cover the buds, opening to magenta-purple with a white central line. The petals are also bright purple, fading to white at the very tip of the spurs. The flowers, which are big for the species, dance on dark purple stems. The young leaves are broadly margined in dusty purple and mature to a dark plain green. The plant eventually grows to 45 cm (18 in.) in height, covering the faded flower stalks.

ZONES 4–8
HEIGHT AND SPREAD 45 × 30 cm (18 × 12 in.)
FLOWERS spring

Epimedium grandiflorum 'Queen Esta'

This cultivar, named for the wife of *Epimedium* enthusiast Harold Epstein, has especially large lavender-pink flowers for the species. They emerge from deep carmine buds in a spectacular fashion that contrasts with the rich purple young leaves. The deep pink sepals are held up above the pale pink petals that conclude in long white spurs. This dramatic plant earns a place either in a pot or in acid leafy soil in any garden. The foliage swiftly matures to a good medium green.

ZONES 5–8
HEIGHT AND SPREAD 30 × 30 cm (12 × 12 in.)
FLOWERS spring

Epimedium grandiflorum 'Spring Wedding'

In 2003 Darrell Probst introduced this delightfully pretty form, which has showers of small pink-and-white flowers that resemble apple blossoms. They are held above the foliage on contrasting long red-brown stems. The detached sepals are palest pink, deepening in the centre over pure white spurred flowers. There is just the faintest hint of pink at the mouth. The foliage is crisp apple green with a distinct maroon margin in spring. The plant is quite low growing.

ZONES 5–8
HEIGHT AND SPREAD 20–30 × 30 cm (9–12 × 12 in.)
FLOWERS spring

Epimedium grandiflorum 'Tama-no-genpei'

This delightful Japanese selection bears rose pink sepals beneath grey-green outer sepals. The inner sepals clasp the pale-pink-and-white petals closely, shading into long white spurs like open talons. The flowers are held above the new leaves, which are tinged purple. The young foliage has slight bronze speckles. The effect is showy, dramatic, and very floriferous. It is said to repeat after the first flush has faded on taller 40 cm (16 in.) stems.

ZONES 4–8
HEIGHT AND SPREAD 15–40 × 23–45 cm (6–16 × 9–18 in.)
FLOWERS spring

Epimedium grandiflorum 'White Queen'

This lovely selection, which bears large white flowers, is perhaps one of the best whites of the *Epimedium grandiflorum* group. The outer sepals and stems are dusky pink, and they set off the pure white inner sepals and long-spurred white petals. The young foliage has spiny pink-tinted margins. The whole is better than the sum of its parts.

ZONES 4–8
HEIGHT AND SPREAD 25–40 × 30 cm (10–16 × 12 in.)
FLOWERS spring

Epimedium grandiflorum 'Yellow Princess'

SYNONYM *Epimedium grandiflorum* 'Kicho'

This is a quite different form of the species, selected for its delicate pale yellow flowers that open from lime green buds. The broad sepals are creamy white over palest sulphur flowers with long white-tipped spurs held down at first opening, then opening horizontally. The light green leaves are fringed and lightly margined red. Despite its small stature, the plant shows up well in a shady corner. It tends to emerge and flower quite late in the season.

ZONES 4–8
HEIGHT AND SPREAD 20 × 30 cm (8 × 12 in.)
FLOWERS late spring

Epimedium grandiflorum 'Yubae'

This plant has generated quite a lot of synonyms. William Stearn noted that it is called *Epimedium grandiflorum* 'Yubae' in Japanese, and it entered Western gardens under this name. However, it has also been listed as various cultivars of *E. grandiflorum*, including 'Crimson Beauty', 'Crimson Queen', 'Red Beauty', 'Red Queen', 'Rose Queen', and *E.* 'Roseum'. Many nurseries list these names as separate plants. Perhaps poetic licence has given rise to the red and rose epithets, and allows this form to differentiate itself from the purple and carmine varieties.

Although not strictly red, its flowers are a uniform bright cerise pink with white tips to the long down-curved spurs. The outer sepals and buds are purple. Its flowers arise over purplish herbaceous foliage that re-emerges bronze-pink in spring and slowly matures to medium green by summer.

ZONES 4–8
HEIGHT AND SPREAD 40 × 45 cm (16 × 18 in.)
FLOWERS spring

Epimedium 'Heavenly Purple' ▸

Torsten Junker of Junker's Nursery in Somerset, England, bred this lovely new epimedium. It was selected as a seedling of *Epimedium fargesii* 'Pink Constellation' for its large flowers held way above the long green leaves in a leggy tangle of pink and purple. The sepals are pale lilac-pink held tightly against the spurs, which seem to extend the sepals to points. The centres of the petals are a uniform deep purple and the long stamens drop out of the middle like a ballerina *en pointe*.

ZONES 4–8
HEIGHT AND SPREAD 60 × 30 cm (24 × 12 in.)
FLOWERS spring

105

Epimedium 'Hina Matsuri'

In Japanese, *hana matsuri* means "flower festival." The name could have been changed in translation. The plant is herbaceous and resembles *Epimedium* ×*youngianum* 'Merlin' in many respects, but it is much paler. Its outer sepals are grey-pink, enclosing deeper pink inner sepals that open to deep rose. The red stems accent the contrast of the buds with the open flowers. The bell-shaped petals are overlaid with just a breath of rose pink and are carried above the emerging dark red leaves. This is an exceptionally pretty plant with very small dimensions.

ZONES 4–8
HEIGHT AND SPREAD 20 × 20 cm (8 × 8 in.)
FLOWERS spring

Epimedium 'Honeybee'

This delightful hybrid started life with Robin White, but Wildside Nursery in Devon, England, is now the primary distributor. The flowers rise well above the mat of long, pointed evergreen leaves on light green stalks. The sepals are palest cream with a breath of red-brown down the centre. The petals have long in-curved spurs that are pale apricot with a slightly darker yellow tip. They become more veined as they reach the middle and then resolve into a chestnut brown mouth, giving the appearance of a flight of fat bumblebees.

ZONES 4–8
HEIGHT AND SPREAD 30 × 30 cm (12 × 12 in.)
FLOWERS spring

108

Epimedium ilicifolium

In 1998 Mikinori Ogisu originally introduced the so-called holly-leaved epimedium from Shaanxi to the West, and Robin White grew it. Darrell Probst re-collected the specimen in 2001 from the steep mountain-sides along the boundary where Sichuan, Hubei, and Shaanxi meet.

As you might imagine, the plant has large, leathery pointed leaves with long spines. The leaves, which are evergreen, are in three parts. As the young leaves re-emerge in spring, they are a shade of light red-green that sets off the flowers well. These are borne in sprays of 25 to 30 individuals on 25-cm (10-in.) stems. The sepals are pale primrose yellow and sit atop the long yellow petals, each spur curled under itself. The flowers are effective against the foliage, which alone would make it well worth placing in a shade garden.

ZONES 4–8
HEIGHT AND SPREAD 25 × 30 cm (10 × 12 in.)
FLOWERS late spring into early summer

Epimedium 'Jean O'Neill'

Peter Chappell and Kevin Hughes raised this lovely new hybrid at Spinners Garden and Nursery in Hampshire, England, from an open-pollinated seed pod of *Epimedium davidii*. The sepals are palest creamy pink and cover the long petals, whose spurs curl in like long legs in yellow boots. The petals resolve into dusty apricot at the mouth around yellow stamens just showing like the tip of a tongue. The flower stems are pale apple green, and the foliage is glossy and prickly.

ZONES 5–8
HEIGHT AND SPREAD 30 × 30 cm (12 × 12 in.)
FLOWERS spring

Epimedium 'Kaguyahime'

This natural hybrid occurred in Yamaguchi's nursery in Japan. Its parents are probably *Epimedium acuminatum* and *E. dolichostemon*, which were growing in neighbouring beds. The name derives from a tenth-century Japanese folk tale about a bamboo cutter who discovers an infant princess in the heart of a glowing bamboo stalk. Its flowers are a striking combination of large rose pink sepals above deep purple petals whose short in-curved spurs resemble a purple baby enclosed by pink bamboo. These attributes on their own make it worth growing. But its most striking feature is its brilliantly coloured young leaves, which are large, spiny, and irregularly splashed oxblood red. The colour combination is showy and dramatic. The second growth flush keeps its spring leaf colour for weeks on end.

ZONES (4)5–8
HEIGHT AND SPREAD 30–45 × 30 cm (12–18 × 12 in.)
FLOWERS spring

Epimedium 'King Prawn'

Julian Sutton bred this pretty and increasingly popular hybrid using Mikinori Ogisu's *Epimedium wushanense* as the pollen parent and *E. latisepalum* as the seed parent. The plant inherits its long well-marked evergreen leaves from the former and its larger flowers from the latter. The plant's colour can vary with the weather, but generally it has pale pink sepals held aloft above the long-spurred petals in the same shade of pink, each with a bright yellow tip that lifts the whole colour scheme. The centre of the petals forms a dark, dusty pink mouth. Tall pale green stems bear the flowers above the new foliage. It is a vigorous and healthy hybrid with a distinct will to live.

ZONES 5–8
HEIGHT AND SPREAD 30–40 × 30 cm (12–16 × 12 in.)
FLOWERS spring

Epimedium 'Kodai Murasaki'

This Japanese hybrid is an impressive plant. It resembles *Epimedium grandiflorum* in leaf, but the flowers are a spectacular shade of Bordeaux red held on tall dark red stems. The purple-black outer sepals enclose the entire buds like blackcurrants. They open to reveal rich cranberry purple sepals held well above the long petals, which are a similar purple and conclude in paler tipped spurs. The mouth of the flowers is a darker shade of purple, and the whole package is set against pale apple green leaves. This is another must-have plant.

ZONES 5–8
HEIGHT AND SPREAD 70 × 30 cm (28 × 12 in.)
FLOWERS spring

Epimedium 'Lastalaica'

Thierry Delabroye has an unerring eye for a good plant. He selected this hybrid for both its dazzling pink young foliage and its lovely lemon yellow flowers. The emerging leaves are long, pointed, and salmon pink, with darker pink splashes and spots. The flower stems are dark purple with markedly purple outer sepals in bud, which open to reveal ivory white inner sepals, lightly dusted with pink, over cream spurs concluding in a butter yellow tip. Towards the central mouth of the flower, the colour coalesces into a lemon yellow margin around darker yellow stamens. The flower is a symphony of pink and yellow, a combination most colourists frown upon, but in this plant it is a triumph.

ZONES 5–8
HEIGHT AND SPREAD 50 × 30 cm (20 × 12 in.)
FLOWERS spring

Epimedium latisepalum

In 1993 Mikinori Ogisu introduced this spectacular plant from Sichuan. The true species has small light green outer sepals on white buds that open to reveal wide white, almost translucent, sepals that are angled up like an inverted parasol. The petals are a subtle mix of primrose yellow and palest pink at the centre, and they resolve into long white spurs with yellow-green tips, which are held horizontally and curve slightly downwards. This plant is similar to, but larger than, pure white *Epimedium ogisui*. The leaves are large, toothed, and roundly pointed, and appear in threes atop tall stems.

However, the species is rather promiscuous in cultivation, and some plants offered for sale seem to be seedlings that have crossed somewhere along the line. It is worth buying the plant in flower to check its authenticity.

ZONES 5–8, might be more tender
HEIGHT AND SPREAD 15–30 × 23–30 cm (6–12 × 9–12 in.)
FLOWERS spring

Epimedium 'Lemon Zest'

Darrell Probst selected this plant as the best seedling from a bed of hundreds that had attracted great interest from his customers. The mound of evergreen foliage renews itself with spiny leaves that are variably marked and splashed with a deep bronze red. Multitudes of dark brown stems rise to 35–40 cm (15–16 in.), carrying sparkling yellow flowers. These have small outer sepals that are stained light red above small butter yellow inner sepals. The petals resemble those of *Epimedium ecalcaratum*, spurless but more rounded.

ZONES 5–8
HEIGHT AND SPREAD 13–15 cm (5–6 in.)
FLOWERS spring

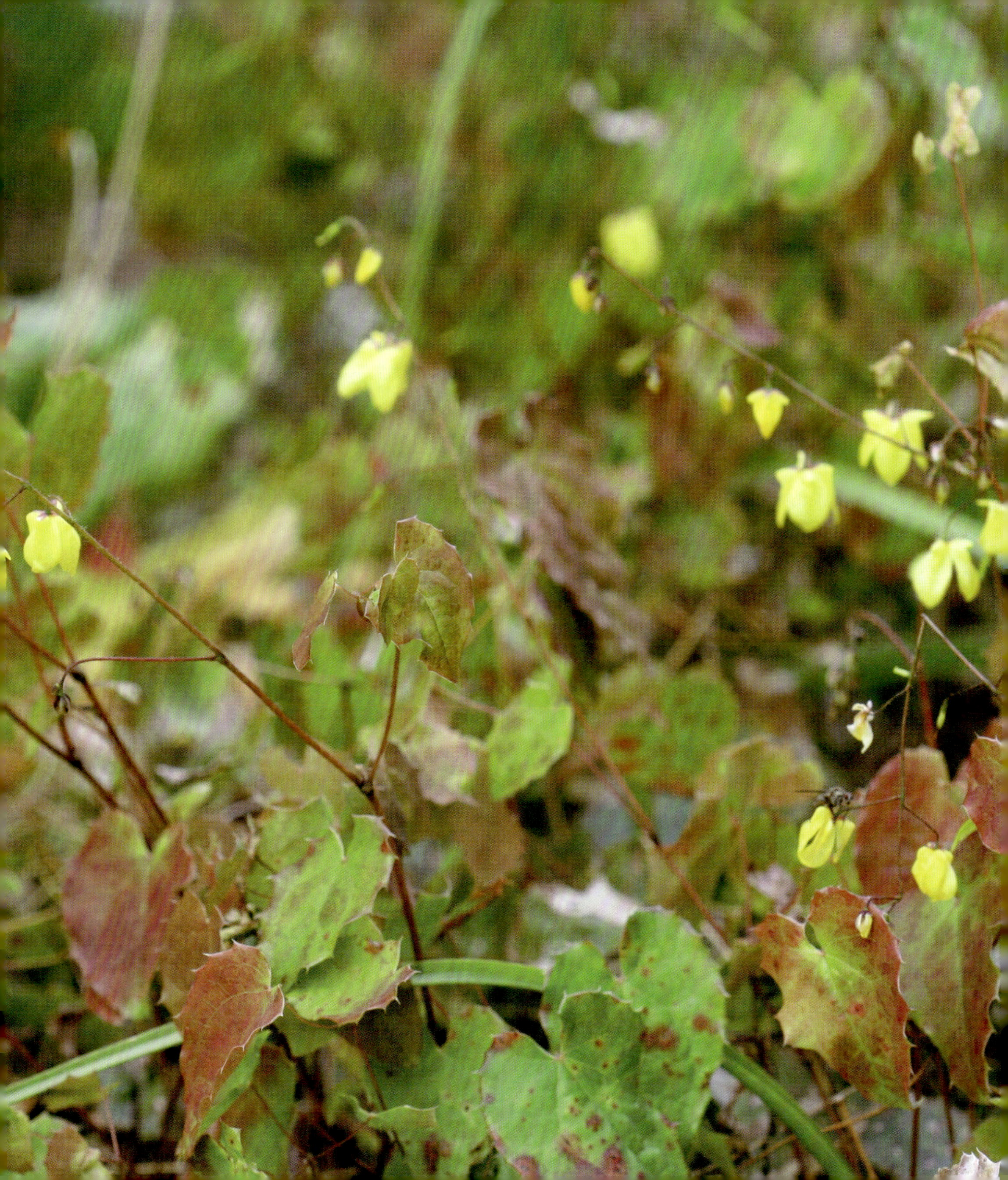

Epimedium leptorrhizum

Although French missionary Émile-Marie Bodinier originally collected this plant in Guizhou at the end of the nineteenth century, it was not correctly identified until the 1930s. It is curious that no one noticed its large pink drooping flowers until Mikinori Ogisu re-introduced it from Sichuan and wowed Western gardeners.

The species is very similar to *Epimedium brachyrrhizum*, but differs in some botanical details. The number of spines on the edge of each leaf of *E. leptorrhizum* is 10 to 13, whereas the former has 17 to 20, and the name refers to the nature of the rhizome. *Epimedium brachyrrhizum* has more compact, clump-forming rhizomes, whereas *E. leptorrhizum* has longer, thinner rhizomes. Most collectors would not need to grow both of such similar species.

The airy flowers comprise large rose pink sepals whose tips are slightly up-tilted. The spurred petals, which are about the same length and also tilt upwards, are a paler shell pink with light yellow tips. The long stamens and prominent anthers are lemon yellow in the centre of each flower, and they resemble the legs of a butterfly landing on a leaf. The evergreen leaves are large, spiny, deeply veined, and pale on the undersides. They are slightly mottled bronze when they first emerge in spring.

This plant needs a moist, but draining and not boggy, soil to ensure its narrow tuberous roots do not dry out. It would be wise to mulch the plant with leaf mould in winter to ensure the roots stay plump and the leaves remain lush and green.

ZONES 5–8
HEIGHT AND SPREAD under 15–20 × 30 cm (6–8 × 12 in.), continues in an ever-widening spread
FLOWERS early spring

Epimedium leptorrhizum 'Mariko'

This selection is well worth growing in its own right. It bears larger flowers with deeper cherry pink sepals, palest pink to white spurred petals beneath, and prominent yellow stamens and anthers. The young leaves are splashed red and pale green. The whole plant is like *Epimedium leptorrhizum* on steroids. 'Mariko' prefers rich, leafy soil in light shade. Mulch in winter with garden compost or leaf mould.

ZONES 5–8
HEIGHT AND SPREAD under 20 × 30 cm (8 × 12 in.), eventually
FLOWERS early spring

Epimedium lishihchenii

Despite its quite unpronounceable name, this species has earned a prominent place in the shade garden. It derives its name from Li Shih-chen (1518–1593), who British scientist Joseph Needham described as "probably the greatest naturalist" in Chinese history and worthy of comparison with the best of his scientific contemporaries in Renaissance Europe.

William Stearn first identified the plant as *Epimedium membranaceum* subsp. *orientale* from the dried specimens held at Kew from various nineteenth-century collections, although he suspected it might prove to be a new species. Mikinori Ogisu brought back fresh specimens in 1996, when he visited the site of its origin in Lusha, Jiangxi, and from these Stearn was able to confirm that it was indeed new.

And what a species. It is evergreen, with softly beige-pink new leaves and others that are lime green in spring edged with iridescent spines. The flowers nestle among the young foliage without being hidden. They are shades of lemon yellow, cream, and darker yellow. The outer sepals are quite small and green, resting on the backs of the limey inner sepals. These, in turn, sit over the long-spurred petals that are pastel yellow with bright yellow tips. The flower stems are light apple green, whereas the leaf stems are slightly pink.

ZONES 4–8
HEIGHT AND SPREAD 45 × 30 cm (18 × 12 in.), may spread more in warmer climates
FLOWERS early spring

Epimedium Magique Elfes Series

Thierry Delabroye has been working on breeding new epimediums, and he has produced a seed strain that he calls Magique Elfes. These plants are sold directly to the public, the name indicating their provenance. They do, of course, vary in their colour, dimensions, time of flowering, and so on, but are all hardy in Zones 4 or 5 through 8.

ZONES (4)5–8
HEIGHT AND SPREAD variable
FLOWERS variable

Epimedium 'Marco'

Daniëlle Monbaliu of Epimedium nursery in Oostkamp, Belgium, introduced this striking hybrid. She spotted it among the seedlings growing in the nursery of Marco van Noort, a renowned Dutch nursery owner. Van Noort breeds and bulks up new varieties of a multitude of plants before launching them on the wholesale market. (Monbaliu has a good eye for a good plant.)

The evergreen foliage re-emerges at the same time as the wine red flowers. The new leaves are long, pointed, and spiny like holly without being painful in any way. They are green with dark red stains and splashes, and they set off the flowers very well. These are held on green-brown stems and have red-pink sepals with a deeper red central band that almost cover the long spurs, which are held horizontally and are a rich cranberry red with light yellow tips to leaven the pink and red. The whole is a very special plant.

ZONES 4–8
HEIGHT AND SPREAD 30 × 30 cm (12 × 12 in.), probably
FLOWERS spring

Epimedium ogisui

This species was named for Mikinori Ogisu, who has been instrumental in introducing so many wonderful new epimediums from Sichuan and Yunnan. This lovely white-flowered species, which he introduced from Sichuan in 1993, is a fitting tribute to his endeavours and reputation. The wide pure white sepals almost cover the spurs entirely. The flowering stems are borne horizontally, and are often among the earliest in the garden to open. The evergreen leaves re-emerge purple and bronze in spring and age to a light green. Although this plant was discovered adjacent to a waterfall in the wild, it does not need to be in a boggy situation. It is perfectly happy in the usual moist but draining humus-rich soil.

ZONES 4–8
HEIGHT AND SPREAD 15–30 × 45–60 cm (6–12 × 18–24 in.)
FLOWERS early to mid-spring

Epimedium ×omeiense 'Akane'

SYNONYM *Epimedium* ×*omeiense* 'Emei Shan'

When Mikinori Ogisu came across a collection of hybrids between *Epimedium acuminatum* and *E. fangii* growing on the sacred Buddhist mountain of Emei Shan (Mount Omei), he discovered plants in a wide range of colours and form. He selected two very different specimens: one he called *E.* ×*omeiense* 'Emei Shan', and the other he named *E.* ×*omeiense* 'Stormcloud'. The former has been re-named *E.* ×*omeiense* 'Akane', which is the Japanese word for red.

The long-stemmed flowers are a complex mixture of vermilion red short sepals over long-spurred petals that have yellow rims at the mouth, meld into orange-red, and fade to a translucent white in the spurs tipped with sharp butter yellow. The effect catches the eye of all who see it. The young foliage of this evergreen is speckled and marbled with bronze that matures to a shining green in summer.

ZONES 5–9
HEIGHT AND SPREAD 35 × 35 cm (14 × 14 in.)
FLOWERS later in spring

Epimedium ×omeiense 'Myriad Years'

This is a truly spectacular selection by U.S. plant-hunter Dan Hinkley. It went out of commerce for a time, but Tony Avent of Plant Delights Nursery in the United States has re-introduced it, and the plant has made its way to Europe. Hinkley found it growing out of limestone cliffs in Sichuan and has since propagated it by division. The flowers have pale lavender-pink sepals large enough to almost cover the deep purple spurred petals that are suspended on long 50 cm (20 in.) arching stalks well above the foliage, which emerges with a distinct pink cast.

ZONES 5–8
HEIGHT AND SPREAD 30 × 100 cm (12 × 40 in.) within a few years
FLOWERS spring

Epimedium ×omeiense 'Razzleberry'

In 2010, Tony Avent introduced this bright-eyed flower, which appears on long arching green stems above mounds of new red-splashed leaves. The large white sepals appear like wings above the deep purple petals. The long spurs are tipped with light yellow, which is repeated around the mouth. 'Razzleberry' was also selected from the naturally occurring hybrids found on Emei Shan (Mount Omei). It spreads slowly and steadily.

ZONES 5–8
HEIGHT AND SPREAD 30 × 30 cm (12 × 12 in.) in foliage, extending to 45 cm (18 in.) in flower
FLOWERS mid- to late spring

Epimedium ×omeiense 'Stormcloud'

The sinister purple-brown and yellow colouring of the flowers seems in direct contrast to *Epimedium ×omeiense* 'Razzleberry'. While 'Stormcloud' may not be showy within the garden, its subtle hues would seize anyone's attention in a terra-cotta pot. The hunch-backed sepals are purple-brown and edged with yellow. They sit astride long in-curved spurred petals that become paler and more translucent, culminating in sharp yellow tips. Towards the centre of the flower, they gradually become suffused with purple-brown, with yellow margins around the mouth.

ZONES 5–9
HEIGHT AND SPREAD 35 × 35 cm (14 × 14 in.)
FLOWERS spring

Epimedium ×*perralchicum* 'Fröhnleiten'

This form bears bright golden yellow inner sepals beneath small beige outer sepals that open wide and are held horizontally. The petals are small and slightly bronze-red in colour, with only vestigial spurs around the central yellow stamens. Heinz Klose selected it in Germany. The plant has long been the favourite of gardeners and garden designers for its tolerance of dry shade under trees, where it spreads to form a large low patch.

Epimedium ×*perralchicum* first appeared in the garden of George Fergusson Wilson at Wisley in Surrey, England, which is now part of the Royal Horticultural Society's headquarters. Wilson had planted *E. perralderianum* close to *E. pinnatum* subsp. *colchicum* at the turn of the twentieth century, and by 1934, according to William Stearn, they had formed a single huge plant with varying forms and flowers. From this mass, three distinct clones were separated. Eighty years later, we now have in commerce only *E.* ×*perralchicum* 'Fröhnleiten'.

The leaves are evergreen, turning bronze-red in winter, and they suppress most weeds. Cut off the leaves in late winter before the flowers start to extend so you can admire their panicles.

ZONES 5–8, evergreen from Zone 6 south
HEIGHT AND SPREAD 35 cm (14 in.), spreading several metres (yards) in all directions
FLOWERS spring

Epimedium perralderianum

Three French botanists discovered this parent of *Epimedium* ×*perralchicum* 'Fröhnleiten' in the mid-nineteenth century during an expedition to northeastern Algeria. This unique area is a remnant of the lowland forest that once extended along the shores of the Mediterranean. The plant was named in memory of Henri René le Tourneaux de la Perraudière, who succumbed to a fever he caught in the region, and died. *Epimedium perralderianum* is very similar to *E.* ×*perralchicum*, with bright yellow sepals over lightly bronzed and yellow petals. It is very tolerant of dry shade.

ZONES 5–8
HEIGHT AND SPREAD 20–25 × 40 cm (8–10 × 16 in.), spreading several metres (yards) in all directions
FLOWERS early spring

Epimedium 'Phoenix'

This is a lovely new hybrid with large pink sepals held up above darker pink petals, with a touch of purple, that conclude in white-tipped spurs held inwards. British enthusiast Wendy Perry selected it from a batch of seedlings of *Epimedium acuminatum* that had probably crossed with *E. grandiflorum*. The foliage is evergreen and lightly splashed with red as the new growth emerges in spring. In winter, the foliage colour turns bronze.

ZONES 5–8
HEIGHT AND SPREAD 20 × 30 cm (8 × 12 in.)
FLOWERS spring

Epimedium 'Pink Champagne'

SYNONYM *Epimedium* 'Elf Orchid'

Darrell Probst considers this glorious epimedium to be among the best hybrids he has selected. It has been sold as 'Elf Orchid', but its true name is more appropriately celebratory. It has a swarm of large leggy flowers held well above the mat of dark mottled foliage. The rose pink sepals lightly rest on the top of the long-spurred petals. These petals are deep strawberry pink at the mouth and fade along the spur to the same colour as the sepals, terminating in a light yellow tip. It is one of the few true pink hybrid epimediums. The evergreen leaves are long, medium green, and arrow shaped, and their purple splashes set off the flowers. This is a vigorous plant with an expansive will to live, and it will repeat flower if it is established and happy.

ZONES 5–8
HEIGHT AND SPREAD 30 × 30 cm (12 × 12 in.), up to 40 cm (16 in.) tall in flower
FLOWERS spring, and may repeat

Epimedium 'Pink Elf'

This hybrid, one of the prettiest of Robin White's introductions, is the result of crossing *Epimedium leptorrhizum* with *E. pubescens* and selecting out this seedling. It bears swarms of tiny two-tone pink flowers held on dark brown wiry stalks above pink-bronze new leaves. The wide shell pink sepals provide a canopy for the spurred petals. They are dark beige-pink about the mouth, fading to pale pink at the end of the long spurs. The plant not only flowers prolifically in early spring, but often repeats the performance at the end of the summer. It is one of the earliest specimens to flower, so wait to cut off the winter leaves until later in spring to give the young buds a little frost protection, especially if the garden is very vulnerable to cold weather. Propagation for re-sale is prohibited.

ZONES 5–8
HEIGHT AND SPREAD 35 × 30 cm (14 × 12 in.)
FLOWERS early to mid-spring, and often repeats in late summer

Epimedium pinnatum subsp. *colchicum*
Colchian barrenwort

Originally, this species was subdivided into different botanical subspecies, but this form has proven to be the survivor in gardens and commerce. It originates in the Black Sea area of the western Caucasus through to northern Iran. It is thus hardy and very drought tolerant, which makes it invaluable for covering the ground in dry, dense shade.

The plant bears bright yellow flowers with rounded sepals and small red-brown petals within that are slightly spurred. The leaves are bronzed in autumn and as they re-emerge in spring. Depending on the locality, the foliage is good and shiny, and more or less evergreen. This is a plant with a great zest for life and growth.

ZONES 5–8, evergreen in warmer zones
HEIGHT AND SPREAD 25 cm (10 in.) to an ever-expanding spread
FLOWERS spring

Epimedium pinnatum subsp. *colchicum* 'Thunderbolt'

Of the few selections of this tough old species, *Epimedium pinnatum* subsp. *colchicum* 'Thunderbolt' is quite the best for its stunning winter foliage. Skip March of the U.S. National Arboretum originally collected the specimen in Soviet Georgia in 1973. Darrell Probst, in conjunction with the Arboretum, named it in 2000.

The plant takes a back seat throughout spring and summer, producing typical yellow flowers on 25-cm (10-in.) stems. With the onset of autumn and winter frosts, the leaves darken to vivid red or, in the right place, near-black, with paler veins standing out in a thunderbolt pattern. Just like the species, this has a terrific will to live and expand. Probst claims that it grows 15–20 cm (6–8 in.) per year. It is a useful introduction that will fill a dry, shady place.

ZONES 5–8
HEIGHT AND SPREAD 25 × 30 cm (10 × 12 in.) and onward
FLOWERS spring

Epimedium platypetalum

This charming species, an early introduction from China in the 1920s, has lemon yellow flowers with no sign of spurs. The flowers hang like small primrose yellow campanulas well above the green spiny leaves. The sepals, which are very small and white, hold the rounded spurless yellow petals. In autumn, the leaves flush purple and remain throughout the winter. The plant usually spreads slowly to form an expanding patch of foliage even in dry shade. Darrell Probst recommends growing it in cracks in stonework or rocks, similar to the habitat where he spotted it growing in the wild. It is a classy addition to a shady garden. The plant spreads slowly by thin rhizomes that are 20–30 cm (8–12 in.) long.

ZONES 5–8
HEIGHT AND SPREAD 25 × 30 cm (10 × 12 in.)
FLOWERS early to late spring, according to seasonal weather

Epimedium 'Red Maximum'

Koen Van Poucke bred this lovely new hybrid at his nursery in western Belgium. He crossed *Epimedium grandiflorum* 'Freya' and *E. membranaceum* to achieve this beautiful evergreen plant. It bears tall light brown stems crowned with sprays of cranberry and rose pink flowers. The outer sepals are dark grey-purple opening to reveal bright pink inner sepals held above long-spurred petals. The mouth of the flower is streaked and suffused pink with a white edge, gradually tapering to translucent white spurs. The young foliage is coloured light brown, turning medium green in summer and winter.

ZONES 5–9
HEIGHT AND SPREAD 30 × 30 cm (12 × 12 in.), until proven otherwise
FLOWERS spring

Epimedium rhizomatosum 'Golden Eagle'

This plant has thin, starkly elegant flowers, with pale pink-flushed outer sepals over cream-coloured inner sepals and long, thin, pale yellow petals that end in long spurs over shiny dark green foliage. It holds its tall sprays of flowers on red stems high above the foliage from early spring, and repeats occasionally throughout the summer. The new young leaves are marked and splashed with red stains before becoming medium green. The rhizome can grow 20–30 cm (8–12 in.) per year.

ZONES 5–8
HEIGHT AND SPREAD 25 × 30 cm (10 × 12 in.), up to 1 m (40 in.) in flower
FLOWERS intermittently from early spring to autumn

Epimedium ×rubrum
Red barrenwort

This plant was originally thought to be the result of a cross between *Epimedium grandiflorum* and *E. alpinum* that was made in the Ghent University Botanic Garden in the mid-nineteenth century. However, Darrell Probst suspected that *E. sempervirens* was a more likely candidate than *E. grandiflorum*, so he made the cross again, and from the resulting seedlings he selected *E.* ×*rubrum* 'Sweetheart'.

Epimedium ×*rubrum* dies down in autumn, going out in a blaze of red. In spring, it again has red young leaves as they emerge. Its flowers are quite small and dainty. The large sepals are dark rose red and cover and enclose the crystal white petals. These are only very slightly spurred, and contrast with the creamy yellow stamens. The whole effect is delicate and pretty.

Grow this selection in shade under trees in neutral soil, as it is not suited to extremes of acidity and alkalinity. It is said to be good in dry shade, but Karen Perkins finds that its leaves go brown in the summer.

ZONES 5–9
HEIGHT AND SPREAD 15–30 × 30–50 cm (6–12 × 12–20 in.)
FLOWERS spring

Epimedium ×rubrum 'Sweetheart'

This plant, together with *Epimedium* ×*rubrum* 'Red Start', is one of a few selections of Darrell Probst's cross of *E. sempervirens* 'Candy Hearts' with *E. alpinum*. It was the first of Darrell's hybrids to be introduced. Crossing 'Candy Hearts' with *E. alpinum* resulted in these plants with flowers that were pinker than those of *E.* ×*rubrum* and with larger, darker, and more heart-shaped leaves that remain more evergreen. The shiny new foliage has a distinct red edge that lifts the whole plant. It is generally more drought tolerant, with good summer foliage with large leaflets eventually reaching up to 40 cm (16 in.) tall.

ZONES 5–9
HEIGHT AND SPREAD 15–30 × 30–50 cm (6–12 × 12–20 in.), up to 40 cm (16 in.) in summer
FLOWERS spring

Epimedium sagittatum 'Warlord'

Darrell Probst selected this named form of the species in 2007. It is grown more for its striking foliage than for its quite small flowers. The evergreen leaves are splashed and spotted in shades of dark red in spring, and they make a darkly attractive background to the clouds of small white flowers with yellow spurs. The long, narrow, pointed leaves are held like the shield of a Roman warrior. The plant makes very slow progress, so it is ideal for a shady corner of a small garden.

ZONES 5–8
HEIGHT AND SPREAD 45 × 30 cm (18 × 12 in.)
FLOWERS spring

Epimedium sempervirens 'Candy Hearts'

This plant is currently available only in the United States, but its shell pink flowers have already found favour with one UK nursery owner, so it is gradually becoming more available in Europe. The sepals and petals emerge from within dusky purple outer sepals on matching purple stems. The flowers crowd out in clusters from among the new leaves, which are attractively edged with opalescent rose pink. The plant is semi-evergreen and prefers acid soil.

ZONES 5–9
HEIGHT AND SPREAD 20 × 35 cm (8 × 14 in.)
FLOWERS spring

Epimedium sempervirens 'Mars'

Like a purple moon-landing vehicle, the strongly coloured flowers on this variety seem to be touching down with their white-tipped spurs. The outer sepals are a smoky shade of grey-purple, opening wide to reveal the cranberry red inner sepals. These sit atop the long spurs, which deepen to a red-purple at the mouth. The whole flower spray is held on red-brown stalks and stands out well from the young foliage. New leaves are bristly and lightly margined with pink. Dick Weaver named the variety from a plant he bought in Japan. The first flush of flowers is soon overtaken by a taller second flush that stands out well above the growing leaves. It is a remarkable plant that is covered in flowers for a long period. It prefers acid soil and produces a second flush of taller sprays up to 25 cm (10 in.).

ZONES 5–9
HEIGHT AND SPREAD 15 × 30 cm (6 × 12 in.)
FLOWERS spring, and repeats

Epimedium sempervirens 'Okuda's White'

This is one of the purest white-flowered forms. The new leaves emerge flushed red-bronze among the large white flowers, which show up to stunning effect. American enthusiast George Schenk introduced it to the West from Japan in the 1970s. Darrell Probst has grown the plant ever since he obtained it in 1995.

It makes neat and tidy ground-cover, and has a more shiny evergreen habit than the rest of its group. Give it a once-over in spring, and trim off any remaining foliage to leave space for the unfurling buds and leaves. In severe winters, the plant sometimes drops its leaves, but it remains hardy. It forms very tight clumps and needs care and a pair of sharp secateurs to divide after flowering. Replant the divisions in acid leafy soil in light shade. Probst recommends mulching the plants in winter in Zone 5 to protect the roots from the worst of winter wet and cold. The rhizome can grow up to 15 cm (6 in. per year).

ZONES 5–9
HEIGHT AND SPREAD 15–20 × 30 cm (6–8 × 12 in.)
FLOWERS spring

Epimedium sempervirens 'Violet Queen'

This is another selection that is starting to become more widely available. However, Darrell Probst states that the naming is quite uncertain. Some suspect it may have been hybridized with *Epimedium grandiflorum*, but it is evergreen. The rounded buds, which are like clenched talons, are enclosed in French grey outer sepals that open to reveal very large purple inner sepals. These are carried over paler petals that are streaked purple and white, and extend to long white spurs. The flowers stand out above the delicate flushed-red young leaves. The plant prefers acid soil.

ZONES 5–9
HEIGHT AND SPREAD 25 × 30 cm (10 × 12 in.)
FLOWERS spring

Epimedium 'Space Wagon'

Thierry Delabroye has selected a plant that really packs a punch. The foliage alone makes this selection worth a place in the front of the border. Its large evergreen leaves are splashed and stained dark purple-red as they re-emerge in spring. The flowers are spectacular. The small sepals are a shouting shade of dark red, a complete contrast to the petals. These have large lemon yellow spurs that gradually darken to gold at the centre, and they are borne in dozens over the mound of foliage. The whole is a masterpiece of Delabroye's making.

ZONES 5–8
HEIGHT AND SPREAD 45 × 45 cm (18 × 18 in.), until proven otherwise
FLOWERS spring

Epimedium 'Spine Tingler'

This striking new selection from Darrell Probst bears lemon yellow flowers that dangle over very dramatic foliage. The small lime green sepals are held like pixies' hats over the spurred petals. These are remarkably long, with dark centres and yellow tips to the spurs. The evergreen leaves are very long, very narrow, and very spiny, and re-emerge splashed bronze and red in spring. The plant is sensationally spine tingling. Note that it is sometimes erroneously named *Epimedium* 'Spinx Twinkler'. Propagation for re-sale is prohibited in Europe.

ZONES 4–8
HEIGHT AND SPREAD 17–25 × 30 cm (7–10 × 12 in.)
FLOWERS early to late spring

Epimedium 'Spinners'

From Peter Chappell of Spinners Garden and Nursery in Hampshire, England, this variety has milky coffee-and-cream-coloured spurred flowers. The sepals are wide and long, and palest creamy pink over petals whose spurs are clawed and terminate in yellow tips that echo the prominent yellow stamens in the centre. They darken towards the central mouth, which is stained beige-pink with light yellow margins. This is a big plant and forms a substantial hillock of evergreen foliage. It is very striking in the shade garden.

ZONES 5–8
HEIGHT AND SPREAD 100 × 30 cm (40 × 12 in.) and more, probably
FLOWERS spring

Epimedium stellulatum 'Wudang Star'

Roy Lancaster first introduced *Epimedium stellulatum* in 1983 from Wudang Shan (Mount Wudang) in Hubei and Sichuan, and described how it filled the cracks between the stones of the ruined Purple Clouds Temple. This species has become known as 'Wudang Star'. Its specific epithet, *stellulatum*, derives from its multitude of white flowers held like a starry cosmos above its light brown new leaves. This clone is the type plant for the species.

Each large white sepal opens horizontally to the stem, exposing the small yellow-brown petals, which are blunt and rounded, and the bright yellow stamens and anthers. The evergreen leaves are toothed and heart-shaped, and you should partially cut them back in late winter to allow the flowers and new foliage to emerge.

ZONES 5–8
HEIGHT AND SPREAD 20–30 × 30 cm (8–12 × 12 in.)
FLOWERS spring

Epimedium stellulatum 'Yukiko'

Mikinori Ogisu made this superbly floriferous selection. It has clouds of wide-open white sepals over a centre comprising a cluster of small bright yellow spurred petals. The flowers stand above the young foliage, which is variably stained light red and bronze over green. It is a lovely selection.

ZONES 5–8
HEIGHT AND SPREAD 30 × 30 cm (12 × 12 in.)
FLOWERS spring

Epimedium 'Sunshowers'

This hybrid originated with Kelly Dodson of Far Reaches Farm, a specialist nursery in Port Townsend, Washington. Dodson passed it on to Darrell Probst, who introduced it in 2008. The plant bears multitudes of pretty pink-and-yellow flowers with veined pink-and-white inner sepals over long-spurred lemon yellow petals. The mouth is deeper yellow, echoing the spur tips. The flowers are held well above the young leaves, which are speckled and loosely margined red. It often repeats its flower along with more young foliage later in the season. It is semi-evergreen and thus loses its leaves in a cold winter.

ZONES 5–9
HEIGHT AND SPREAD 50 × 30 cm (20 × 12 in.)
FLOWERS spring

Epimedium 'The Giant'

This exceptional plant is still quite rare in commerce, but becoming more common. Darrell Probst first discovered it in 2001 growing near Chongqing, Sichuan. It was named for its ability to keep producing new flowers from existing nodes on ever-taller stems. It bears very large, long, spiny, evergreen leaves that are plain green in spring, with a few light brown spots. The flowers arise well above the clump of foliage on long-branching green stems that can reach more than 2 m (6 ft.). They are large, with long pale yellow spurs that have a bright chocolate brown mouth with prominent yellow anthers, and they repeat all season. As a foliage plant alone, it earns its place in the shade garden. It has reached Thierry Delabroye's nursery and is beginning to play a part in his breeding work.

ZONES 5–9
HEIGHT AND SPREAD 90–120 × 30 cm (36–48 × 12 in.)
FLOWERS spring

Epimedium ×*versicolor* 'Cherry Tart'

The flowers of this plant have a distinctly cheeky appearance. They are clear pink with big rounded sepals that are streaked pink and white. Within lie the true petals, which are bright pink with a clear yellow centre around prominent yellow stamens. They have a gamin, fresh look that suggests an enthusiasm for life. The semi-evergreen young leaves have a brown-purple blush in spring and age to mustard yellow in autumn. This chance seedling was discovered in the garden of Judy Springer of Great Falls, Virginia, who gave a plant to Darrell Probst. The parentage is unknown and difficult to guess. The plant spreads slowly by 5- to 10-cm (2- to 4-in.) rhizomes.

ZONES 5–9
HEIGHT AND SPREAD 30–38 cm (12–15 in.)
FLOWERS spring

Epimedium ×versicolor 'Cupreum'

As a distinctly useful plant in dry shade, 'Cupreum' differs from 'Discolor' in the colour of its sepals and the angularity of its leaflets. The sepals are a stronger shade of light coral-pink, and the short-spurred petals are lemon yellow. The whole is very pretty. The evergreen foliage turns a rich mahogany in winter. It looks delicate but is one of the hardiest and toughest plants around.

ZONES 5–9
HEIGHT AND SPREAD 30 × 30 cm (12 × 12 in.) and spreading
FLOWERS spring

Epimedium ×*versicolor* 'Discolor'

SYNONYM *Epimedium* ×*versicolor* 'Versicolor'

Epimedium ×*versicolor* is an early hybrid of *E. grandiflorum* and *E. pinnatum* subsp. *colchicum*. Nineteenth-century botanist Andre Donkelaar crossed the plants at the Ghent University Botanic Garden after Philipp Franz von Siebold brought them over from Japan. This cross produced three named forms: 'Discolor' (originally called 'Versicolor'), 'Sulphureum', and 'Neosulphureum'. 'Cupreum' and 'Strawberry Blush' have joined them.

'Discolor' is much more delicately coloured than 'Cupreum', but just as hardy and tough. According to William Stearn, it differs from 'Sulphureum' in the "conspicuous red colouring of its young foliage . . . and its rose coloured sepals." Stearn also considered it to be deciduous, but in mild gardens and mild winters it appears to be semi-evergreen. In colder climates, the leaves become shabby and die back, but it certainly makes very pretty ground-cover in dryish shade.

ZONES 5–9
HEIGHT AND SPREAD 30 × 30 cm (12 × 12 in.) and spreading
FLOWERS spring

Epimedium ×*versicolor* 'Neosulphureum'

This plant resembles *Epimedium* ×*versicolor* 'Sulphureum' very closely in flower, height, and habit, but it flowers two weeks later in Zones 5 and 6, and is not quite such a spreader. The foliage seems to be more reliably evergreen than *E.* ×*versicolor* 'Discolor', but it makes good groundcover in dryish shade once it is established. 'Neosulphureum' bears clouds of two-tone primrose yellow flowers. The milky cream sepals are rounded and large. They cover the pale yellow flowers, which bear short, stumpy grey-pink spurs that gradually become suffused with primrose. The flower stem is bright green. The spring foliage is more light brown than the red-netted leaves of 'Sulphureum'. The plant spreads slowly by 5- to 10-cm (2- to 4-in.) rhizomes.

ZONES 5–9
HEIGHT AND SPREAD 30 × 30 cm (12 × 12 in.)
FLOWERS spring

Epimedium ×*versicolor* 'Strawberry Blush'

Darrell Probst introduced this particularly pretty form, which has pale pink sepals streaked with rose pink over short lemon and rose pink in-curved petals. The colours are set off by the pink mottling and dark pink margins of the spring foliage. The leaves mature to a handsome dark glossy green. This semi-evergreen plant is particularly drought tolerant.

ZONES 5–9
HEIGHT AND SPREAD 25 × 30 cm (10 × 12 in.) and spreading
FLOWERS spring

Epimedium ×*warleyense*
Warley epimedium

At the turn of the twentieth century, plant enthusiast Ellen Willmott had a large garden at Warley Place, Brentwood, in Essex, England. Here she indulged her passion for roses and many other perennials. She did not stint on the expense, and she was well known for her generosity. When visiting friends' gardens, she would surreptitiously sprinkle seeds of a biennial sea holly (*Eryngium*), subsequently named 'Miss Willmott's Ghost'. When the seeds came up the following year, the garden owners knew they had earned Willmott's approval. After her death, she left behind a legacy of great plants, including a naturally occurring hybrid of *Epimedium alpinum* and *E. pinnatum* subsp. *colchicum*, which was named after her garden.

This distinctive plant is evergreen, making a carpet of bronze leaves in winter, and it bears clouds of small orange flowers in spring above the unfurling new leaves. The rounded sepals stand wide-eyed around the small yellow petals that surround prominent bright yellow stamens. The foliage becomes greener in summer.

Cut off the over-wintered foliage in late winter before the new growth and flower stems unfurl so you can better display them. This is another useful plant for dry shade under trees. It will grow slowly but steadily on 13- to 15-cm (5- to 6-cm) rhizomes.

ZONES 4–8
HEIGHT AND SPREAD 30 × 30 cm (12 × 12 in.), and more
FLOWERS spring

Epimedium 'Wildside Ruby'

Keith Wiley of Wildside Nursery has made a winning choice with his *Epimedium* 'Wildside Ruby'. Individually the flowers are pretty, but their effect against the red young foliage takes the whole plant to a new level. It is an electric combination. The sprays of flower arise on black stems well above the leaves. The outer sepals are a quiet grey, but they open to reveal pink pointed sepals that are spotted and streaked with darker pink. The almost spurless petals are butter yellow and spark the plant into life. But the red young leaves really draw everyone's attention. They are large, pointed, and shiny, and they slowly calm down to plain green. This plant is sure to go far and capture every gardener's eye.

ZONES 4–8
HEIGHT AND SPREAD 30 × 30 cm (12 × 12 in.) and spreading
FLOWERS spring

Epimedium 'William Stearn'

As befits the stature of the late William Stearn's reputation, this is a magnificent plant. Robin White selected it as a seedling from a cross between *Epimedium membranaceum* and *E.* ×*omeiense*. It bears flowers with unusual rich mulberry red sepals over similarly coloured petals that terminate in pale pink and yellow-tipped spurs. The foliage is evergreen, and as it re-emerges in spring the new leaves are mottled and splashed an equally dark red. The effect is gorgeous and dramatic. It is not a vigorous variety, but it is outstandingly lovely.

ZONES 4–8
HEIGHT AND SPREAD 18–30 × 30 cm (7–12 × 12 in.)
FLOWERS spring

Epimedium 'Windfire'

A tangle of jet black stems gives this hybrid a distinct personality. Darrell Probst bred and introduced it in 2007. The flowers also have a burned appearance with their small scorched purple-black sepals over bright butter yellow spurred petals. They are carried well above the mat of green heart-shaped leaves like sparks from a fire. The foliage is semi-evergreen. It is a striking selection and gently spreads by 10-cm (4-in.) rhizomes.

ZONES 5–9
HEIGHT AND SPREAD 30–50 × 30 cm (12–20 × 12 in.) in flower
FLOWERS spring

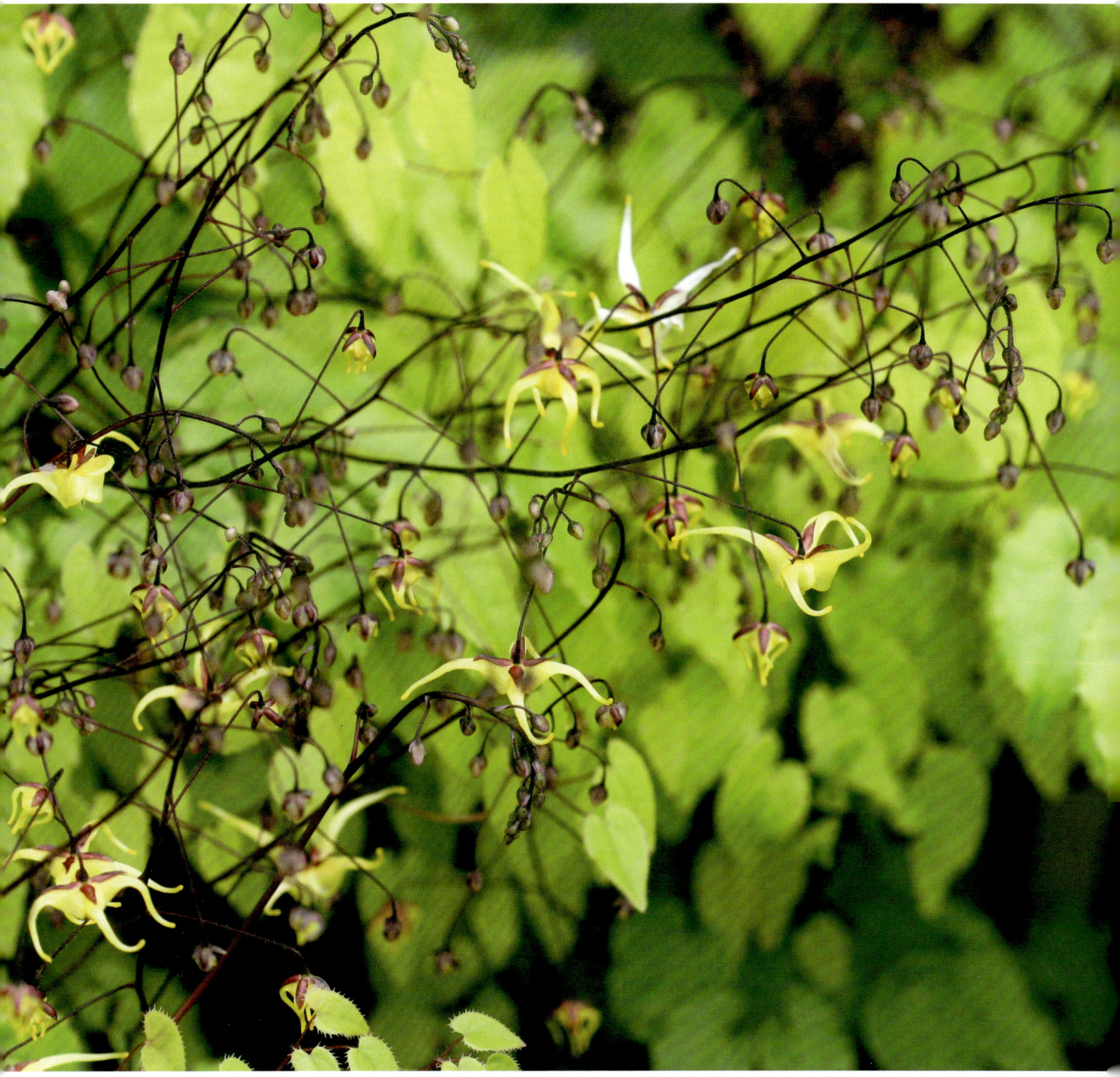

Epimedium wushanense

Chinese botanist Ying Tsün-shen named this species after the mountain Wu Shan in Sichuan when he originally surveyed the Chinese epimediums in 1975. Mikinori Ogisu collected a subsequent specimen in Wanyuan, Chongqing, Sichuan. The plant has grown and impressed gardeners in the United States and Europe ever since it reached commerce. However, there is some doubt over its identity.

The form that Ogisu selected, *Epimedium wushanense* Ogisu's form ▶, has spectacular foliage with long, narrow, elongated, toothed leaves that subtend huge panicles of large flowers. But the other form in commerce currently, *E. wushanense* spiny-leaved form ◀, has swarms of pale yellow flowers on green stems. The large sepals are just a shade lighter primrose yellow than the spurred petals. The young foliage is splashed and marked purple-brown before maturing to medium green.

This plant would make anyone stop and take a second look. Its enormous leaves are long, pointed, and spiny, and when young they have a bronze-pink cast. But the flowers are very different from Ogisu's form. They are big, cluster together tightly in the spray, and arch over on green stems, probably as a result of their weight. The spike of flower reaches up to 60 cm (24 in.) above the huge mound of foliage.

The whole plant would make an excellent subject for a large pot, as the remarkable foliage would carry it through the non-flowering months. Darrell Probst sold many clones under the name "spiny leaved forms" that more or less resemble each other. All are remarkable garden plants.

ZONES 5–8
HEIGHT AND SPREAD up to 130 × 30 cm (48 × 12 in.)
FLOWERS late spring

Epimedium wushanense 'Caramel'

This stunning selection of the Ogisu species is quite different from its apparent brothers and sisters. Darrell Probst and many other experts claim this form is not a true selection of *Epimedium wushanense*. Perhaps it should be more correctly named *Epimedium* 'Caramel'. As the name suggests, it has delicious caramel-coloured flowers with pale cream sepals suffused with light red, and large-spurred light yellow petals with a distinct purple edge around the mouth. The foliage is not quite as dramatic as that of *E. wushanense*, but it is among the best in the genus with long, spiny, narrow leaves that emerge in spring splashed purple-brown. It is quite a specimen plant for rich soil in light shade.

ZONES 5–8
HEIGHT AND SPREAD up to 130 × 30 cm (48 × 12 in.)
FLOWERS late spring

Epimedium 'Yōkihi'

This lovely Japanese selection results from a cross between *Epimedium davidii* and *E. grandiflorum* 'Yubae'. It is a very pretty and vigorous red-, cream-, and white-flowered hybrid. Its flowers are held above the foliage on light green stems with a hint of red. They have rose red sepals held horizontally over white spurs with light yellow tips. The petals become creamy yellow towards the mouth of the flower.

ZONES 4–8
HEIGHT AND SPREAD 30 × 45 cm (12 × 18 in.)
FLOWERS spring

Epimedium ×youngianum 'Azusa'

'Azusa' bears large bright white flowers with long spurs. The stems and outer sepals are red. The deep green herbaceous foliage has a striking silver overlay along the main veins that lasts all summer. It prefers acid soil.

ZONES 4–8
HEIGHT AND SPREAD 18 cm (7 in.) tall in flower, to 30 cm (12 in.) in the second flush
FLOWERS spring

Epimedium ×youngianum 'Be My Valentine'

Darrell Probst named this pretty selection in 1999 in honour of the late Betty Valentine of Berlin, Connecticut, on the occasion of her 100th birthday. She had a passion for epimediums and grew them most of her life. This small gem flowers at 15 cm (6 in.) and extends up to the princely height of 25 cm (10 in.). The flowers are rose pink and white on palest pink stems that positively smother the mounds of young emerging foliage. The sepals are deep rose with a white starry centre, and the petals bear very small white spurs that become suffused with rose pink towards the mouth. It is herbaceous and prefers acid soil.

ZONES 4–8
HEIGHT AND SPREAD 25 × 20 cm (10 × 8 in.)
FLOWERS spring

Epimedium ×*youngianum* 'Fairy Dust'

This delicately stippled lavender-pink selection has great charm. Darrell Probst introduced it in 2004. The base colour is pure white at the centre of the sepals, echoed in the tiny spurs and gradually becoming lavender-pink towards the mouth. The flowers are held above the pale grey-brown new leaves, which seem to be semi-evergreen. It is particularly drought tolerant and prefers acid soil.

ZONES 4–8
HEIGHT AND SPREAD 25 × 20 cm (10 × 8 in.)
FLOWERS spring

Epimedium ×*youngianum* 'Merlin'

This plant arose as a seedling in the garden of English *Epimedium* enthusiast Amy Doncaster, and then was passed to Elizabeth Strangman. Like its namesake, this plant has charm. Its flowers have spurless deep purple sepals with white centres covering the inner pink petals, which hang down like little rounded tassels. They arise quite late in spring above bronze foliage that colours in autumn before dying back. It clumps up well in acid soil.

ZONES 5–9
HEIGHT AND SPREAD 25–30 × 30 cm (10–12 × 12 in.)
FLOWERS spring

Epimedium ×youngianum 'Niveum'

Snowy barrenwort

As its name suggests, this plant bears entirely white flowers with more open sepals that stand up and away from the petals, as well as tiny white spurs. It has a dainty hovering presence like a cloud of snowflakes. The blooms float on dark stems above herbaceous foliage that is lightly flushed and veined red in spring. It grows sturdily in humus-rich acid soil without becoming invasive.

ZONES 5–9
HEIGHT AND SPREAD 25 × 30 cm (10 × 12 in.)
FLOWERS spring

Epimedium ×youngianum 'Purple Heart'

In 2000 Darrell Probst introduced this hybrid, the result of crossing *Epimedium grandiflorum* var. *violaceum* with *E.* ×*youngianum* 'Pink Star'. The plant is semi-evergreen with bright red-purple new leaves that stand out in the border. These deepen as they age, becoming black-purple, and provide a dramatic background to the flowers. The small blossoms are pale pink and white, and they dance above all that purple on tall red stems. The pink sepals arch over the small white petals as if to protect them from the blaze beneath. The herbaceous leaves eventually become green, and in a good autumn they fade back to red-purple. The plant prefers acid soil.

ZONES 5–9
HEIGHT AND SPREAD 25 × 30 cm (10 × 12 in.)
FLOWERS spring

Epimedium ×youngianum 'Tamabotan'

The name means dragonfly in Japanese, although the flowers more closely resemble moths. The seemingly double pendulous bells, both sepals and petals, are pale lavender. They comprise lightly stippled mauve-pink-on-white sepals over white-spurred petals that make loose open mouths with the same mauve-pink in stipples. The dark purple stems hold the little flowers above the dusky purple new foliage. As the flowers die back, the leaves become greener. The plant is herbaceous and prefers acid soil.

ZONES 5–8
HEIGHT AND SPREAD 20 × 30 cm (8 × 12 in.)
FLOWERS spring

Epimedium ×youngianum 'Yenomoto'

This is another form, slightly more pink, where the white flowers with wide open inner sepals arise from tight buds enclosed in dusky pink outer sepals, hanging straight down from pink-red stems. Heart-shaped herbaceous green leaves set off the flowers well. It is happiest in humus-rich, acid soils, and shows up well in light shade.

ZONES 5–9
HEIGHT AND SPREAD 25 × 30 cm (10 × 12 in.)
FLOWERS spring

Epimedium zhushanense

This species is a native of Hubei. The young leaves are bronze as they emerge in spring, with distinctive hairy reverses. The flowers have pale grey-pink sepals and long-spurred pink petals that are the same grey-pink at the tips, becoming suffused with a light purple towards the wide mouth. The stamens are prominent and light primrose yellow. The plant spreads slowly and steadily by 10- to 20-cm (4- to 9-in.) rhizomes.

ZONES 5–9
HEIGHT AND SPREAD 45 × 30 cm (18 × 12 in.)
FLOWERS late spring

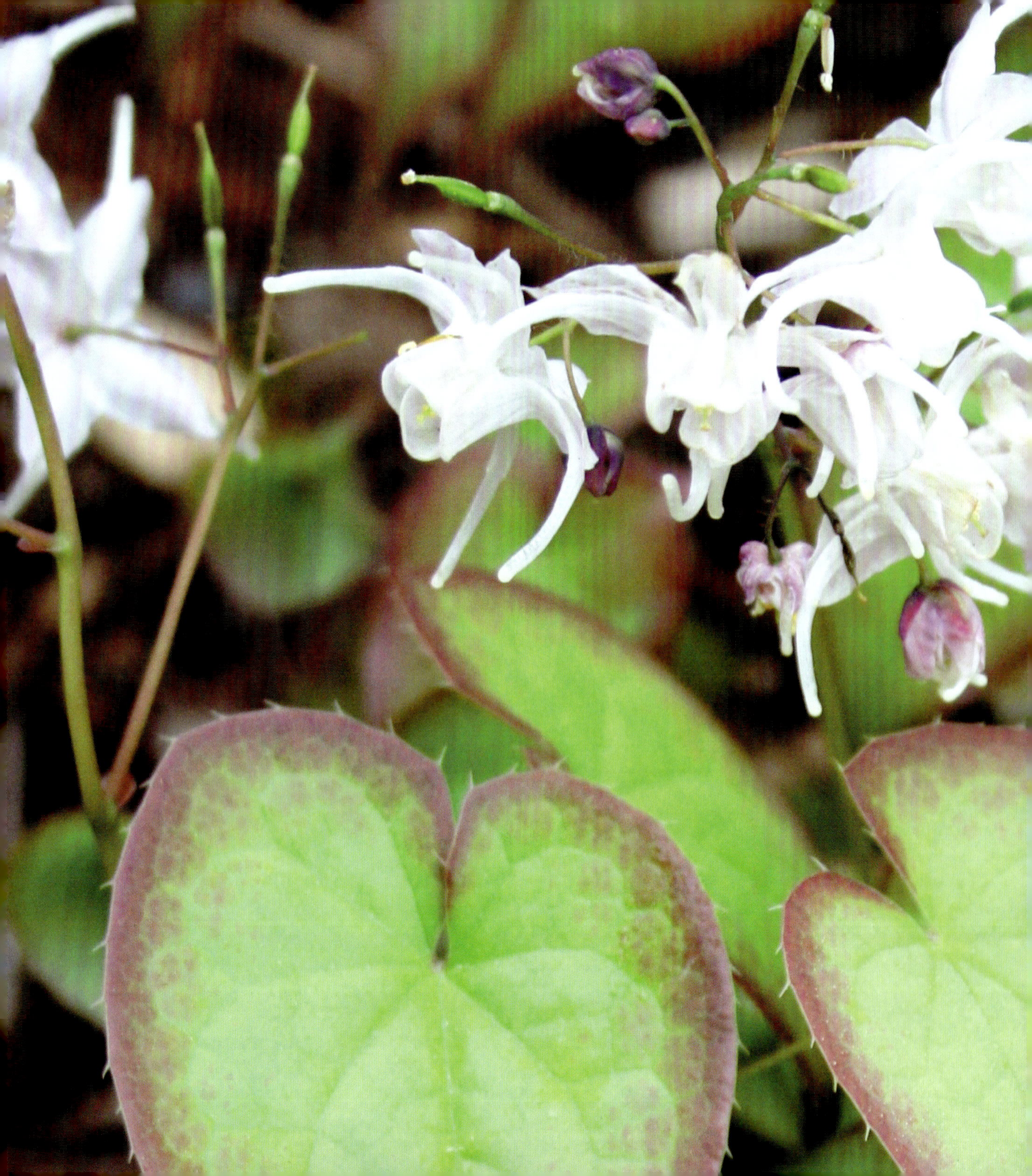

GROWING AND PROPAGATING

Covering this type of structure with suitable creepers, such as clematis and roses, takes just two or three years before there is enough dappled shade to suit epimediums and other shade-loving perennials.

In a very small garden, the shady side of a shrub could play host to one or two epimediums. Roses also cast shade throughout the summer, and the bronzed leaves of the evergreen species of *Epimedium* would make colourful petticoats in winter.

In older gardens that have been neglected, trees and shrubs may have been allowed to grow randomly and the ground beneath might be overgrown. Trees, especially garden trees, need a regimen of good maintenance. Before planting anything in their shade, you need to clear their trunks of side shoots, keep their tops in shape, and remove brambles and invasive weeds from their roots.

Fallen leaves make a terrific mulch for *Epimedium* ×*rubrum*. As the leaves slowly break down, they release much-needed nutrients into the ground.

Bluebells and red-leaved *Epimedium acuminatum* brighten a shady spot in the garden.

Epimediums growing in the shade of shrubs.

Improving the Soil

All epimediums, even drought-tolerant ones, prefer to be planted in soil that has been improved with plenty of well-rotted leaf mould. Garden compost is almost as good, but it can be very alkaline. Most home-made compost has a pH between 8.5 and 9.5, and this material will steadily raise the pH of the garden soil. It is very suitable for growing vegetables, but not for the rest of the garden. After a few years the alkalinity will start to lock up certain soil nutrients, such as iron and aluminum, and will make them unavailable to most plants.

In older gardens, the soil often becomes stagnant, infertile, and poorly drained. When generations of children run and play on the lawn, they create impaction. Epimediums dislike heavy soil that holds water, so aerate this type of space by incorporating horticultural grit and organic matter.

Around a new home, building debris and run-off from the cement mortar wall can cause soil to become alkaline, even if it is initially acidic. Check the pH before you plant any acid-lovers, especially in an area close to a wall.

Leaf mould is nature's gold dust. It is the natural way that nutrients recycle themselves and keep woodland soil fertile and well drained—without raising its pH. In natural woodland there are no mulches or compost bins. Every autumn a tree's leaves fall within

Traditional leaf mould bins in North Somerset, England.

its root-run, mostly around the drip line to a shallow depth. The leaves break down slowly and release their nutrients by spring, when the tree is ready to take them up again.

The traditional method of storing leaf mould is in large compost bins at least 1 m by 1 m by 1 m (40 in. × 40 in. × 40 in.). The leaves rot down over winter.

Colin Crosbie, curator of the Royal Horticultural Society Garden Wisley in Surrey, England, has his own way of creating effective leaf mould. In autumn, he assembles a bin out of large-mesh chicken wire. He stakes each corner of the bin to make the largest possible rectangular area. He then collects fallen leaves and tips them into the bin to a maximum depth of 30 cm (12 in.), as they need to remain relatively dry in order to form a crumbly matter. (If the mix is too wet it becomes slimy and anaerobic—that is, without oxygen—and is unusable.) The leaf mould is ready to use by spring.

Before purchasing plants for your garden, determine whether your soil is alkaline or acidic. You can do this by measuring soil pH, but sometimes it is simpler to have a look at what grows well in your neighbours' gardens. Spaces with healthy stands of camellias, rhododendrons, and summer heathers, and with blue hydrangea flowers, have acid soils. Alkaline soil grows good carnations, sycamore, yew, and clematis, and its hydrangeas are pink. Those lucky enough to garden on neutral soil can grow most things, and their hydrangeas are both pink and blue.

Young leaves of *Epimedium versicolor* 'Sulphureum', an excellent weed-suppressing ground-cover, are well marked with rich red veining in spring.

The majority of epimediums, including most of the new varieties coming in from China and their hybrids, grow well in alkaline soil. All they need are the usual requirements of summer shade and good, fertile soil that drains rather than stays wet and soggy.

Hybrids and selections of the Japanese species, such as *Epimedium grandiflorum*, *E. sempervirens*, *E.* ×*versicolor*, and *E.* ×*youngianum*, prefer acidic soil with a pH between 5 and 7. If your soil is more alkaline, you may be tempted to adjust the pH to grow acid-loving plants.

One way to grow acid-loving epimediums in a garden of alkaline soil is to raise a bed above ground level and fill it with known acid soil. Lighten any heavy loam with well-rotted leaf mould, and be prepared to keep filling it up as the soil drains into the garden beneath. (Past recommendations might have mentioned adding bales of peat, but now that we have become more aware of the damage to peat bogs and their habitat, this is no longer an option.)

Digging down into alkaline soil and replacing it with known acid soil is a more temporary solution: in five or six years the invading alkaline ground water will push up the pH reading. (Soil water actually determines the pH.) Lining the hole with a membrane does not really help, as the alkaline water will still penetrate from outside eventually.

It is more satisfactory to plant out the epimediums that are happy in alkaline soils, and pot up the acid-lovers in ericaceous compost. They will grow for a few years this way, and then perhaps you could split them up in summer and re-pot them.

It is important to water potted plants with rainwater. A barrel to collect the run-off from the greenhouse or the roof would be ideal. Make sure to keep the container covered: dead mice and rotting leaves are not good for plants. In the absence of rainwater, use cold boiled water, and

The dramatic *Epimedium grandiflorum* 'Queen Esta' earns a place in either a pot or acid leafy soil in the garden.

Slightly acidifying a neutral or slightly lime-y soil

COLIN CROSBIE DISCOVERED that the naturally slightly acid soil in his garden was becoming steadily more alkaline with the use of hard water and alkaline garden compost. He began mulching the soil with bracken or composted bark. This material gradually lowers the pH by perhaps a degree over the course of 10 years.

always be prepared to add some sequestered iron (sold in the United Kingdom as Sequestrene) to help the absorption of iron.

Planting

If you are planting just one or two epimediums into an existing shady border, excavate a larger and deeper hole than the size of the plant container. Fork leaf mould into the bottom layer of the planting hole, and add some into the excavated soil waiting on the side.

If the soil is dry, pour at least 2 litres (0.5 gallon) of water into the hole with a watering can. Use rainwater for the lime-hating species. This will help the roots to establish themselves in the damp ground. Place the plant in the hole at the same depth it was in its pot, or slightly deeper. If you leave any of the rootball above the level of the surrounding soil it will act as a wick and dry out the roots.

Put back the topsoil first, improved with more organic matter, and use your heel to firm it down. Replace the remainder on top until the hole is slightly overfilled.

Water the plant again to settle the soil around it. Finally, mulch it with a layer of leaf mould to retain the moisture. Mulch newly planted epimediums every winter thereafter, but take care not to put on mulch to a depth greater than 5 cm (2 in.). A deep mulch can cause plant roots to come to the surface and subsequently dry out faster.

In the first summer after planting, it pays to give each plant at least 2 litres (0.5 gallon) of water when the weather is very dry just to keep the plants growing. They will settle down much more quickly.

Digging a large hole for a newly acquired epimedium.

Heeling in a newly planted epimedium.

Maintenance

Once well planted, epimediums require little care. They are easy plants that do well in the shady parts of the garden with very little attention, but some basic maintenance helps.

A minority of epimediums, including the Japanese species and their crosses as well as several other species and hybrids, are completely herbaceous. You should tidy up their leaves and stalks in early winter and perhaps cover the the plants with a light mulch of leaf mould for protection.

The majority of epimediums, however, are evergreen and lose their leaves only in a very severe winter. By late winter and into very early spring, evergreen foliage can begin to look rather tatty. Winter weather takes its toll, and early spring sunshine peers into those winter dark places and highlights the brown edges, the holes, and the tired leaf colour.

Choose a mild weather spell before you start cutting off the over-wintered leaves of the vigorous weed-suppressing varieties, such as *Epimedium pinnatum*, *E. ×versicolor*,

Use shears to cut off over-wintered foliage of vigorous evergreen epimediums in late winter.

Herbaceous Epimediums

Epimedium 'Akebono'
Epimedium 'Alabaster'
Epimedium 'Beni-kujaku'
Epimedium 'Flowers of Sulphur'
Epimedium grandiflorum and selections
Epimedium 'Hina Matsuri'
Epimedium 'Yōkihi'
Epimedium ×youngianum and selections

and *E.* ×*perralchicum*. These are tough enough to attack with a pair of shears. Clip off all the leaves well before the new young growth has started to extend, as nothing is more frustrating than inadvertently cutting off flower buds before they have even begun. This practice will enable the flowers to open well and clearly, and the new leaves will set them off with panache, uncluttered by the tired old foliage.

It is better to tidy up the somewhat less vigorous new evergreen varieties with a pair of sharp secateurs once spring has begun. Take care not to cut off the unfurling new stems. Leaving some of the winter foliage gives the emerging flower buds a little protection, as heavy late frosts can damage their soft young stems once they have sprung into life.

One of the most important jobs is to cut off the seed pods before they release their seed. Any seed produced within a garden will have hybridized with its neighbours, and the resulting plants will not be the same as the parent. Such hybridization will also occur in a nursery where more than one species is grown. Sometimes the seeds fall down within the crown of the parent plant and corrupt it. If you are buying a beautiful named variety, be sure the nursery grower cut off the seed pods before they were ripe, and try to buy a plant in flower so you can check its identity.

In late winter, snip off the damaged foliage but leave most of the over-wintered leaves.

Growing Epimediums in Pots and Containers

Gardens are getting increasingly smaller in this modern world. At one time, every house would have been built with a garden for children to play on the grass, for growing vegetables, and for relaxing with friends. Now there are constraints of smaller areas for building and additional profit for builders, and garden space is usually the first casualty. In many countries throughout the world, more people are living in cities where the only outdoor space is a balcony or even a window box, so pots and containers fulfil an important function. Whereas the more vigorous spreading forms of *Epimedium* are not entirely suitable for containers, the smaller Japanese plants and the new Chinese species and their hybrids are ideal.

Epimedium 'Kaguyahime' growing in a pot in my nursery.

Epimediums for Containers

Epimedium 'Egret'
Epimedium 'Flowers of Sulphur'
Epimedium grandiflorum 'Queen Esta'
Epimedium 'Kaguyahime'
Epimedium 'Lemon Zest'
Epimedium ×*omeiense* 'Akane'
Epimedium 'Persian Carpet'
Epimedium 'William Stearn'

The long-stemmed bi-coloured flowers of *Epimedium* ×*omeiense* 'Akane' deserve the close-up inspection they get when grown in a container.

In early spring epimediums start to push up their flowers and renew their leaves, and by mid- to late spring the whole pot is inspirational. Many of these lovely new plants have exquisite blooms that demand a closer look, so growing them at eye level is ideal. One or two of the epimediums with browner, redder foliage are enhanced by a terra-cotta container, whereas they might be somewhat ignored in the border.

Some Japanese epimediums prefer acidic soil, so if your garden is decidedly alkaline, planting them in pots offers the opportunity to enjoy their charms. Likewise, a few of the calcicole species that have a distinct preference for alkaline conditions can be accommodated in a pot of proprietary compost with slow-release nutrients. (Dressing the soil with lime has only a temporary effect and needs to be repeated frequently.)

Winter colour.

PREPARING CONTAINERS

Prepare your container during the winter, long before the epimediums have even thought of flowering. Choose a pot that will accommodate the plant comfortably, or one that is much bigger to allow for planting companions.

Fill half the container with proprietary compost, either acid or alkaline, and add the correct dose of a slow-release fertilizer or a well-balanced organic mixed fertilizer. Once you have mixed fertilizer into the compost, it is important to use it within four weeks, before the nutrients begin to leach out.

Plant the epimedium in the compost so the pot is filled to a level just below the rim. This will allow the compost to settle when it is watered. Then put in any other companion plants and fill the gaps with more compost. Tap the pot down, or shake it about if it is not too heavy, to settle the compost roughly. Top it up again if necessary.

When the pot is filled, move it to its eventual site. Water it thoroughly with a watering can with a rose attached so as not to make holes in the compost.

Insert plant labels so you don't forget what you have planted. And lift the pot onto pot supports to prevent bugs, beasties, and slugs from invading the drainage holes.

CHOOSING COMPANION PLANTS

Depending on which epimedium you have chosen and whether it has good evergreen foliage, you might consider planting some companions for winter or for later in the summer. Many of the plants listed in this section would make excellent companions, but some might be too big, too fleeting, or a little too bare for winter.

Evergreen grasses make excellent companions, especially for winter. *Acorus gramineus* 'Ogon' could be a little too brightly yellow, but it would look good with a sparkling yellow-flowered epimedium, such as *Epimedium* 'Lemon Zest'. Bowles' golden grass (*Milium effusum* 'Aureum') is a lighter shade of lemon yellow. It sets off beautifully some of the lovely palest cream-flowered forms, such as *E.* 'Flowers of Sulphur' or *E.* 'Egret'.

Neatly striped *Carex conica* 'Snowline' teams up well with some bright blue scillas and the apricot pink *Epimedium* 'Persian Carpet'. And, although not really a grass, but a member of the asparagus family (Asparagaceae), black grass (*Ophiopogon planiscapus* 'Nigrescens') sets off all and sundry very well, including *E.* 'Egret'.

In larger containers, upright bronze *Carex buchananii* or *C. flagellifera* that arches over would complement any of the brighter orange- or red-flowered epimediums, such as *Epimedium* 'William Stearn' or *E.* ×*omeiense* 'Akane'.

The world population of heucheras increases year after year, with ever more astonishing leaf colours and flowers, all of them evergreen. Many make excellent winter partners for potted epimediums. Many tiarellas have been crossed with heucheras to create the hybrid ×*Heucherella*, and the best of these combine the handsome foliage of heuchera with the tall, pointed pink flowers of tiarella. Any of these would be small enough, and reliably evergreen, to combine in a pot with any epimedium.

Smaller semi-evergreen ferns, such as hart's tongue (*Asplenium*), are ideal associates for a larger container, as would be *Polystichum setiferum* in all its forms. Dwarf *Dryopteris affinis* 'Crispa Gracilis' has tightly curled fronds that look like someone has squeezed them dry.

Epimedium 'Persian Carpet', *Carex conica* 'Snowline', and blue scillas in a pot in my garden.

Ypsilandra thibetica in a pot among the epimediums.

Extending the season of interest after epimediums have flowered in their pots is a matter of choosing from myriad summer- and autumn-flowering plants. But sometimes placing another pot for an alternative season is better than trying to cram everything into the same container.

Subjects for separate but compatible containers could be chosen from among late winter and early spring perennials such as *Ypsilandra thibetica*. This would be hardy in most gardens and self contained enough for a pot.

MAINTAINING CONTAINERS

Putting a plant in a pot makes that plant the centre of attention, so it needs to be in tip-top condition all the time. Therefore it is important in spring to tidy up any leaves that have deteriorated during the winter, perhaps leaving just one or two leaves to protect the delicate emerging flowers and young foliage from the worst of the winter weather. Note that green leaves are still photosynthesizing and thus feeding the plant, so refrain from chopping off the lot. With deciduous species, clear away all the dead leaves as soon as they have lost their autumn brightness.

Even with potted epimediums, one of the most important tasks in early summer is to remove the seed pods before they burst and spread their seeds. They are very promiscuous. At the same time, tidy and maintain any potted partners so the whole container always looks fresh and well cared for, even into the depths of winter.

Gardeners ask a lot of their plants by growing them in pots and letting them stand through the freezing wet of winter. Their roots are just the thickness of the pot walls away from the extremes of cold. In very low sub-zero temperatures, especially after a period of rain, the wet plants' roots can freeze and die. If your container is standing in an exposed place when the worst of the freezing winter winds and snow arrive, move it into a cold greenhouse or a garage. Take it out again when the cold abates, or it could be forced into growth—and then will be even more vulnerable to later frosts.

In some years British garden designer Dan Pearson discovers that especially freezing easterly winds in early spring have seriously damaged his plants in pots. This is a problem with container-grown epimediums. Covering them with horticultural fleece and leaving the over-wintered foliage intact can provide extra protection. Nonetheless, Pearson finds that epimediums planted in the ground tend to fare better.

Propagation

Epimediums are self-sterile. This means that each individual plant is unable to pollinate itself, and that as a group epimediums ensure their genetic diversity. Bees do most of the pollination, which has to be between two plants.

These two plants can be from the same species or from different ones. In wild populations individual species grow in one place, so their progeny is also of that particular

In cultivation, *Epimedium acuminatum* and *E. dolichostemon* have hybridized to produce *E.* 'Kaguyahime', seen here with *Pulmonaria* 'Blue Ensign'.

species. But sometimes two or three different species grow together or within the radius of a bee's flight, and some naturally occurring hybrids occur between the species. This has undoubtedly taken place on Emei Shan (Mount Omei).

In plant nurseries and gardens we tend to grow different species and cultivars quite close together. So any seed is almost certainly the result of a cross between the parent plant of one species and its neighbours of different species. Consequently, seed that is set in a garden or nursery is rarely true to the parent plant species. It will be, by definition, different.

Seed pods and blossoms on *Epimedium* 'Flowers of Sulphur'.

PROPAGATION BY SEED

If you can be quite sure there are no other species of *Epimedium* within a bee flight of a particular plant, you are safe to sow the seed as it is set. The seedlings will be variants of the parent species. However, a bee forages for up to 6.5 kilometers (4 miles), so in the majority of cases you can assume that self-sterile epimediums will cross with some neighbour somewhere. Your seedlings will then be different from the parent. You could

The red-mottled leaves of Epimedium 'Artanis', one of Thierry Delabroye's hybrids, complement the spotted foliage of the aptly named Podophyllum versipelle 'Spotty Dotty'.

try your hand at breeding a new cultivar, but beware of introducing another plant that is very similar to one that is already in cultivation. It only results in confusion.

In some nurseries, such as Tony Avent's Plant Delights, stock plants are not protected from pollinating bees. The resulting seedlings are lifted, lined out, and selected at the flowering stage.

In others, such as Pépinières Delabroye, the best of Thierry Delabroye's own hand-crossed hybrids are grown to flowering stage in polytunnels, netted to keep out the bees, then selected to provide the parents of deliberate crosses. From these second-generation crosses the best are chosen and named. Delabroye created his Magique Elfes Series in this way.

Collect and sow seed as soon as it is ripe. This may sound easy, but the seed pods ripen willy-nilly, and they can split quite suddenly and release the very small seeds onto the ground beneath.

According to Darrell Probst, seed usually takes about 45 days to set from the time the flowers were pollinated. This is useful information if you are making deliberate crosses.

The seed then needs 60 days below 4°C (39°F) to break down the inhibitors and germinate. This is best accomplished in a domestic refrigerator at its lowest setting, or you can leave the seed tray outside in a shady spot to weather over the winter. The frosts should do the work, and the seed will likely germinate the following spring.

Alternatively, set a potted plant on a shaded seed bed of sharp sand and a little loam. The seeds should fall down and germinate in their own time in the seed bed. But beware of weeds, mice, birds, slugs, and snails. They are all after the seed for themselves. Put some netting over the seed bed and use slug preventative to deter the slimy ones.

PROPAGATION BY DIVISION

As epimediums grow larger, and perhaps out-grow their allotted space, gardeners' minds often turn to dividing them. If you have dead-headed the plant and prevented seedlings from growing within the crown, it is quite safe to lift the whole plant and divide it up. Robin White liked to divide all his epimediums in midsummer.

Karen Perkins separates epimediums into different camps for dividing: evergreen and herbaceous; clump-forming or spreading by rhizomes. She lifts the evergreen varieties between early summer and early autumn, after the new foliage has hardened off but while the soil is still warm and the new roots can grow away. She lifts the deciduous varieties just after the buds re-emerge in spring, and she has also had success in autumn.

Karen chooses a cool, cloudy day to divide her plants. Using a serrated knife or a spade, she divides the clump-forming varieties, then cuts off rooted rhizomes of the running forms with secateurs. The roots can be cut back to 10 cm (4 in.) to re-invigorate them. She cuts back the top growth by about a third, especially of those varieties with big leaves, such as *Epimedium wushanense*. This reduces the moisture loss from the foliage while the roots are getting re-established.

Divide a clump-former with a serrated knife.

Epimedium rhizomes.

Plant out divisions in their final positions, or pot them up and place them in a cool, shaded environment where they can make plenty of new roots and re-establish very quickly. In the latter case, keep them in a garden frame over the winter and plant them out the following spring. Remember to keep them shaded and watered at all times, and watch out for vine weevils, which love peaty and leaf mould–rich soils.

Pests and Diseases

Epimediums are tough, easy-to-grow plants with wiry stems, shiny evergreen leaves, and good resistance to most of the pests and diseases that our gardens throw at them. But there are a few nasties out there lying in wait for your precious plantings.

It is always wise to try to resolve pest and disease problems without resorting to chemicals. If your only recourse is to use insecticides and fungicides, rotate your brands and make sure each one has a different active chemical constituent. This practice will go some way towards preventing the build-up of pest resistance to a particular product.

VINE WEEVILS

Vine weevils are evil beasts. They are a special problem for potted epimediums. They particularly like peat-based composts, and appear to be on the increase in gardens. Try a loam-based potting compost or one of the new peat-alternative mixtures. You can also avoid containers altogether, as vine weevils feast less frequently on epimediums growing in the garden.

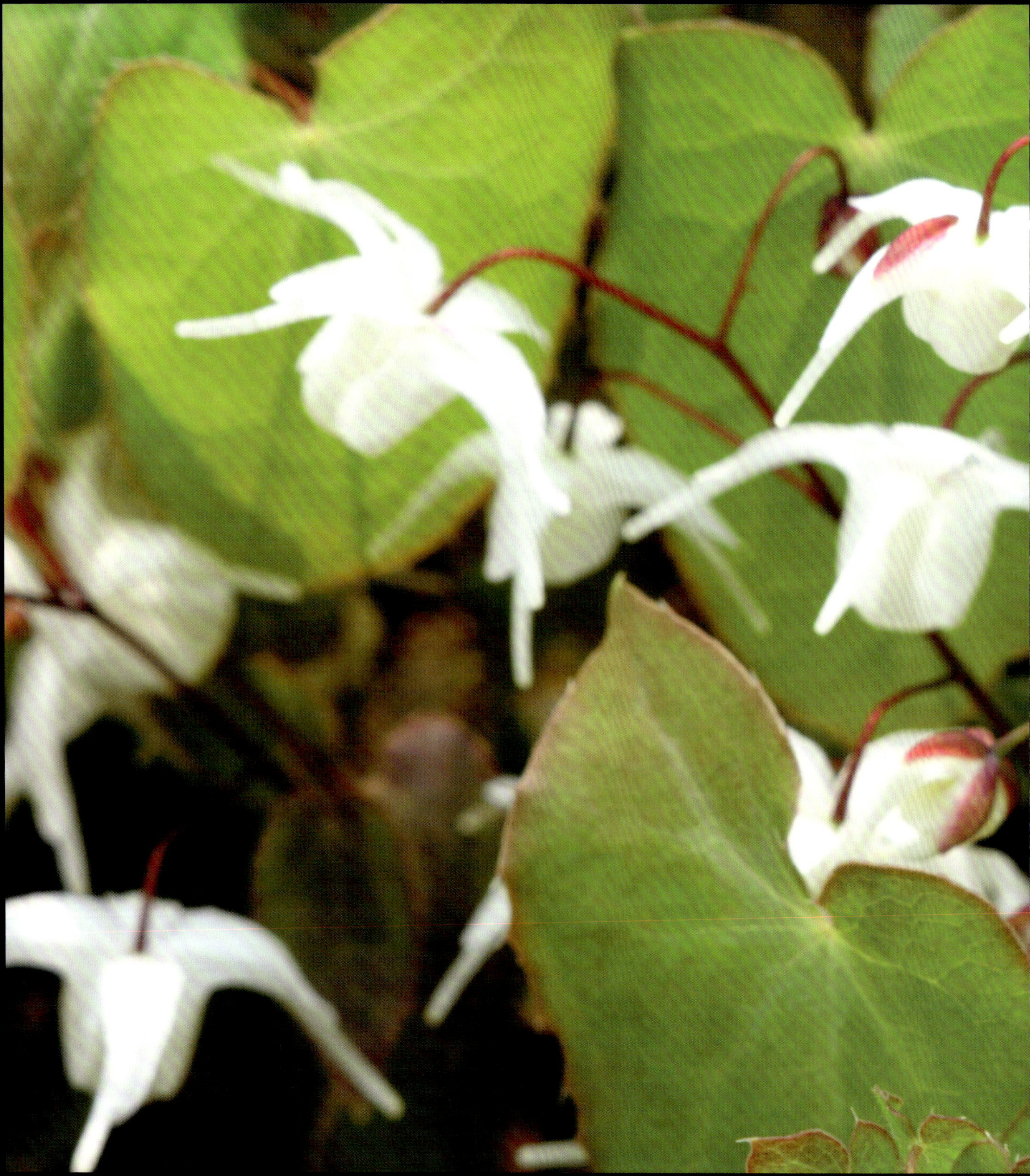

PEOPLE, PLACES, AND PLANTS

E

Epimediums come from the mountainous woodlands of China, Japan, and central Europe, and the Constantine mountains of northeastern Algeria. There are about 50 recognized species. China is a treasure trove of new *Epimedium* species, far outnumbering those from any other country. The only limitation is lack of access for vehicles into remote areas, but it can only be a matter of time before many more species are discovered.

The genus *Epimedium* belongs to Berberidaceae, the berberis family. Gardeners are familiar with the shrubby members of this family such as barberry (*Berberis*), *Mahonia*, heavenly bamboo (*Nandina*), and the bi-generic cross ×*Mahoberberis*. However, there are many more, if rarely grown, herbaceous genera, including *Achlys*, *Bongardia*, *Caulophyllum*, *Diphylleia*, *Gymnospermium*, *Jeffersonia*, *Leontice*, *Podophyllum*, *Ranzania*, and the more familiar *Vancouveria*. The grouping is quite loose, with each genus sharing one or two characteristics. Botanists are still trying to organize them.

Epimedium alpinum, the first epimedium grown in a European garden.

Early Cultivation of Epimediums

The first epimedium to claim the attention of first-century Greek herbalist Dioscorides was a small, low-growing plant with leaves like ivy, few if any flowers, and roots that gave off an unpleasant smell when crushed. He named the plant *Epimedion* after the country of the Medes, southwest of the Caspian Sea. The exact species remains unknown: Dioscorides' writings were long copied and translated, leading to corruptions in the texts, so the precise identity of this plant has been lost in the convolutions of time.

However, during the sixteenth century just such a plant was found growing in the woods around Vicenza, Italy. It was collected and introduced into cultivation, first within Italy and then steadily throughout Europe. London herbalist John Gerard called the plant *barrenwort*, alluding to its possible herbal use as a contraceptive.

Swedish botanist Carl Linnaeus received barrenwort from Empress Catherine the Great of Russia, and he grew it in his so-called Siberian garden at Hammarby near Uppsala. Linnaeus named the plant *Epimedium alpinum* in 1753. It was the only *Epimedium* species known in Europe and became the genotype for the genus.

A woodland ground-cover tapestry composed of *Jeffersonia, Smilacina, Vancouveria, Sanguinaria* (bloodroot), and *Epimedium*.

Epimedium perralderianum has been growing in British gardens since 1862. It is named after Henri René le Tourneaux de la Perraudière, who collected it in Algeria in the nineteenth century. The plant grows in the Constantine mountains, a unique area among the hot deserts of the southern coastline of the Mediterranean. The weather in the region is cool and wet, with snow falling during the winter, although in summer there is very little rain. In such conditions this species thrives. It has become one of the classic plants for dry shade.

Medicinal Uses and Conservation Issues

Over the ages, herbalists have disagreed about the medicinal use of epimediums. Whereas Dioscorides recommended the plant's roots as a contraceptive when ground into a paste and mixed with wine, Roman Pliny the Elder noted that it had "thickening and cooling" properties and that women should avoid it.

John Gerard stated, "This rare and strange plant was sent to me from the French King's Herbarist, Robinus, dwelling in Paris at the signe of the blacke head, in the streete called Du bout du monde [the end of the world]." It does not sound very respectable. Perhaps the plants' alleged contraceptive properties were useful to disreputable inhabitants.

However, the other common names—horny goat weed, rowdy lamb herb, randy beef grass—seem to imply an aphrodisiac effect, and in China the plant is thought to be a natural form of Viagra, perhaps encouraged by the story of the goat herder who noticed an increase in sexual enthusiasm among his flock after they had eaten epimediums.

Modern scientists have analyzed the chemical make-up of *Epimedium* and found that one of its constituents acts against an enzyme that restricts the flow of blood to the penis (technically known as a phosphodiesterase inhibitor). *Epimedium* might be an herbal remedy for erectile dysfunction with only mild side effects, but as yet it is untested, and experts cannot yet condone its safe use or work out proper dosages. The side effects are largely undocumented.

Large quantities of epimediums are collected in the wild in China. For centuries gardeners have cut the leaves of *Epimedium sagittatum* and dried them for sale as Ying

Epimedium sagittatum growing in the wild in Xiuning county in east China's Anhui province.

Yang Huo, or organic Viagra. However, more recently harvesters have started to uproot entire plants. This practice endangers the continuity of the wild plant and its environment. *Epimedium* enthusiasts should object to this and should not purchase wild-collected plants. Otherwise, this species—and many others that could be mistaken for it—will simply die out.

Introducing Japanese Epimediums to Cultivation

In 1775, Philipp Franz von Siebold was seconded as a physician to the Dutch East India Company in Japan. He was given quarters on the tiny island of Deshima just off the city of Nagasaki. This extraordinary man-made island was created as a way of barring foreigners from mainland Japan while maintaining a viable trading base with the West.

Keeping strangers at arm's length was important to the Japanese rulers, or Shōgun. The Portuguese had tried to introduce Christianity to Japan in earlier times. They brought in missionaries and bibles, which proved very unpopular with the Shōgun. When the Dutch opened trading negotiations, they were also suspected of being Christians. "But," they declared, "We are not Christian. We are Dutch!"

Von Siebold was German. The Japanese had granted trading rights only to the Dutch company, so he had to convince them he too was Dutch. When asked about his different accent, he asserted that he was a "mountain Dutchman." The Japanese were appeased.

Von Siebold soon became entranced with everything he saw. The foreign inhabitants were hardly permitted to leave Deshima, but occasionally von Siebold's fascination with the flora of Japan overcame the prohibitions. He lectured on Western medicine to an enthralled audience, and eventually the ailing Shōgun sought his advice. Von Siebold made the journey to the ruler's bedside with eyes peeled for unusual plants he passed on the way. On his return to Deshima, he acquired a goat. Little grew on Deshima, so von Siebold's manservant had to travel to the mainland to acquire the vegetation the goat needed. Von Siebold gradually built up a large collection of Japanese plants in all their variety. He employed local artist Kawahar Keiga to paint his *Epimedium grandiflorum* and *E. diphyllum*, which provided a firm, transportable record to take home.

During his five-year stay on Deshima, von Siebold also fell in love with a young Japanese woman named Taki. He and Taki set up home together, and she bore him a daughter, Ine. Von Siebold had no plans to leave the island, but he was so keen to explore Japan that he got his hands on some maps through illegal means. This was a capital offence. When the Shōgun found out, he had von Siebold arrested. Instead of ordering von Siebold's execution, the Shōgun honoured their friendship and handed down a more lenient sentence of immediate deportation.

Von Siebold, heartbroken by the termination of his life with Taki and Ine and devastated at leaving the richness of the Japanese flora, packed up 1200 plants and set sail for Europe. During the long voyage the majority of the plants died: just 260 epimediums survived and found a home in the rich soils of the Ghent University Botanic Garden in present-day Belgium.

The Ghent University Botanic Garden has been the point of first introduction for many *Epimedium* species, as well as the Japanese species von Siebold brought over. Since early times Ghent botanists have worked on classifying and naming these epimediums correctly, and over the years the garden has become a repository for the different species. The type plants, examples from which other members of a species can be compared, catalogued, and identified, were sent at first to the Botanic Garden at Kew and are now held in Ghent. Chinese botanist and collector Chen Yi and the Japanese collector Kawarada have also sent type plants, and Ghent holds the plants collected by Mikinori Ogisu via Robin White.

Additionally, Darrell Probst has offered specimens of plants collected in the wild to director Paul Goetghebeur to see if he could name them. Many of these unique plants might possibly be species new to Western botany. Scientists have studied these epimediums, but the results are technical and complicated, and outside the scope of this book.

The collection at Ghent is divided into three parts. There is a shade tunnel that acts as a quarantine area for newly arrived plants. They are established in raised beds and kept free of pests and diseases, then either planted up outside or kept in the tunnel for study.

There is also a border in the shade of the glasshouse that receives plenty of light, but not direct sunshine. The bed is raised at the back to give the plants good drainage in classic moist but draining soil. This border is open to the public, as is the arboretum where epimediums are included in plantings where possible.

The research is ongoing. Marc Libert oversees the now-vast collection of epimediums held in Ghent. He rationalizes the species and forms within the collection, which is a Herculean task, given that it is very important to have the correct botanical description, pictures, and references of each species.

Libert has also selected two hybrids. One is *Epimedium membranaceum* crossed with an unidentified parent. It has red-orange flowers and bears the name 'Ghent Orange'. Like its known parent, it has a continuous flowering habit. The other is called *E.* 'Rik'. It has been selected from a sowing of seeds from *E.* ×*omeiense* 'Akane' that belongs to enthusiast Rik Van Bogaert, a colleague at Ghent University with a wonderful private collection. The very colourful yellow-and-red flowers look rather smiley, according to

The beds at Ghent University Botanic Garden in Belgium.

Epimedium 'Rik' is named for enthusiast Rik Van Bogaert.

Libert. They appear in large numbers and dance over the well-marked leaves. *Epimedium* 'Rik' may go into commercial production in Holland in the near future. It is clear that Libert has a good eye for a distinctive hybrid.

Establishing Order Out of Chaos

New species of *Epimedium* continue to be discovered and planted out in botanic gardens throughout Europe, and sometimes they are confused and misnamed. At first little was understood about the plant's determination to hybridize readily between species, and chaos reigned from the end of the eighteenth century into the early twentieth century. Professor William Stearn began to take an interest in epimediums in the 1930s. He gathered dried specimens from all over Europe, observed living plants in 22 botanic and private gardens, and concluded that many "species" bore two or more names, and that there were no examples of some of these "species" growing in the wild. Either they had disappeared (improbable in what are often remote parts of the world) or, more likely, they had hybridized in cultivation.

In 1958 Stearn published a paper in the *Journal of the Linnean Society of London* that identified 23 species of *Epimedium*, including 10 subordinate categories and 11 distinct hybrids. No book on the subject of epimediums could be written without mention of Stearn. His work *The Genus Epimedium* is the bible on the subject.

Stearn was an exceptional communicator as well as a distinguished plantsman. He wore his learning lightly, and he could explain anything to anyone. Roy Lancaster recalls talking about botanical nomenclature over lunch with Stearn shortly before his death. Stearn pointed to the knives and forks laid out before him and remarked how similar they were to plant nomenclature. Collectively, they were all cutlery; that is their family name. And within the cutlery family there were knives, forks, and spoons, or the genera. The

Epimediums and hellebores in a border.

four members of the spoon genus—serving spoon, dessert spoon, soup spoon, and teaspoon—are the species. And if each of the spoons had individual names engraved on their handles, these would be the cultivar names.

Stearn completed his account of *Epimedium* and *Vancouveria* shortly before he passed away in May 2001. Alas, he did not live to see its publication. Since his death, however, plant-hunters have increased the number of species introduced into cultivation many times over. Stearn would have been delighted to see how many wonderful plants have been discovered, hybridized, and selected.

Introducing Chinese Epimediums to the World

When Mao's Cultural Revolution slowly lost its grip on the country, many of the more remote parts of China became accessible to botanists. In 1975, Tsün-shen Ying wrote a paper identifying 13 *Epimedium* species hitherto unknown in the West, and Mikinori Ogisu visited the remote valleys of China. He and Roy Lancaster collected an amazing number of new species and naturally occurring hybrids. Ogisu, other Chinese authors, and Stearn subsequently identified another 29 species new to Western horticulture. Before he died in 2001, Stearn put the total number at 54 species.

In the 1980s and 1990s, Ogisu discovered 11 *Epimedium* species new to botany and six that were already known but not yet grown in gardens. Botanists and gardeners owe a great debt to Ogisu for searching for, collecting, and introducing new epimediums and plenty of other plants. He discovered, catalogued, and photographed many entirely new species in the wild valleys of some of the remotest parts of China, and he continues to do so. According to Lancaster, Ogisu assures the botanical world that he "will look even harder for new species" to bring into cultivation.

Epimedium ogisui, named in honour of Mikinori Ogisu.

Among the epimediums Ogisu has introduced, two are named for him: *Epimedium mikinorii*, an evergreen plant with bright white sepals and deep brown-purple spurred petals, and *E. ogisui*, a fine white-flowered form.

Roy Lancaster accompanied Ogisu on expeditions to Sichuan and became a friend and first point of contact in the United Kingdom. Lancaster was a member of Ogisu's 1993 expedition to Sichuan, which brought back so many new species.

In particular Lancaster recalls finding a pure white-flowered form with starry flowers with yellow extremities. It was growing in rocks outside the Purple Clouds Temple on Wudang Shan (Mount Wudang) in Hubei province. Lancaster collected five seeds, which he gave to Robin White. Only one germinated, and eventually it produced clouds of pure white starry flowers with bright yellow extremities. Lancaster named it *Epimedium stellulatum* 'Wudang Star' after the mountain on which it was found. He was also responsible for the discovery and introduction of *E. acuminatum* 'Galaxy' in 1993, with creamy white sepals and spurs and a beige-yellow centre.

Often when Ogisu returned on his own with seed and samples, he would take them to show to Lancaster in Hampshire, England. Lancaster recalls "the excitement of his visits and the unwrapping of bare-rooted seedlings on the floor of our sitting room." These were passed on primarily to White to be propagated and used in breeding hybrids.

Lancaster also remembers "first making known Ogisu's discoveries to Professor Stearn" and then taking Ogisu to meet Stearn at Kew, "where we spent a most amazing day examining Ogisu's photographs, drawings and plants, which is what persuaded the professor to go ahead and write his book on the genus."

Darrell Probst, who has discovered four previously unknown species and re-introduced another, has also made three expeditions to Sichuan and other remote parts of China and returned with collections of more species. The first trip was in 1996 to Yunnan with Dan Hinkley, Tony Avent, and nine other enthusiasts. They studied dried specimens beforehand and targeted promising areas to visit, as well as lesser-known areas with suitable terrain that were likely to contain interesting new species. The group was limited to 30 days in China, and they endured the frustration of waiting for roads to be repaired or being turned back where they were still under construction, and learning that bridges had been washed away.

One of the species Probst discovered is *Epimedium wushanense*, which he collected from Wu Shan (Mount Wu) in 2004. It has huge evergreen leaves that make an outstanding clump crowned with clusters of pastel yellow-cream flowers in spring. This plant is very different from the one Mikinori Ogisu collected 400–500 kilometers (200–300 miles) away from the known area of distribution of *E. wushanense*.

Marc Libert agrees. He states:

[G]oing back to the basic description it is very clear that all types of the Ogisu collections are clearly not *E. wushanense*. The real thing is a very distinct plant that we grow (in Ghent) in four introductions, one even of a blueish tone.

The basic difference lies in the dense panicle of the true *Epimedium wushanense*, which is known in Belgium as *Syringa epimedium*. The plant that Ogisu collected has

Epimedium stellulatum 'Wudang Star', named for the mountain on which it was discovered.

much looser panicles. In the true form, the flower is broad, rather than elongated, as it is in Ogisu's type.

Libert feels it is hard to know into which species *Epimedium wushanense* 'Caramel' should be integrated. It could fall into the group known as *E.* 'The Giant', but it does not definitively seem to belong to *E. wushanense* (an opinion he shares with Probst).

Epimedium wushanense at Wanyuan, North Chongqing, Sichuan.

Flowers of the spiny-leaved form of *Epimedium wushanense* growing today in Belgium.

The First Hybridists of the New Chinese Species

As new species were brought to the West, plant breeders were eager to start crossing them and "improving" the flower forms, the leaf colour, the habit, the size, and the time of flowering. In the United Kingdom, Roy Lancaster passed on new species to Robin White to make deliberate crosses, selecting those that were special from the widely varying seedlings being grown.

White is skilled at germinating epimediums from seed, and second to none at propagating them for sale. With the exception of *Epimedium acuminatum* and *E. stellulatum* 'Wudang Star', which came straight from Roy Lancaster, most of the species were from Mikinori Ogisu, who wanted to get them to Stearn for the revised monograph. White already had a working relationship with Lancaster, who knew of his interest in anything new. They arranged that White would establish anything that Ogisu collected and then pass the material on to Stearn.

White was also responsible for some of the best new hybrids introduced in the United Kingdom and further afield. Some were from deliberate crosses, while others were spontaneous. He grew hundreds of seedlings to flowering, but demonstrated the ruthless judgement of a successful plant breeder, as 99.9 percent of them ended up on the compost heap, even though they were beautiful. *Epimedium* 'Amber Queen', however, was deliberately bred to flower for a long period and to hold its flowers well above the foliage. A very different sibling, *E.* 'Golden Showers', was also selected, but it was not commercialized until a year or so before White's nursery closed. Other selections included *E.* 'Arctic Wings', *E.* 'Fire Dragon', and *E.* 'William Stearn'. All are long flowering, given the right conditions. The same can be said for *E.* 'Flowers of Sulphur', *E.* 'Star Cloud', *E.* 'Mme Butterfly', and the remarkable *E.* 'Pink Elf'.

Blackthorn Nursery is now closed, but White distributed many of his epimediums with a Plant Breeders' Rights tag that ensures high propagation numbers. Most are easily available from specialist nurseries.

Epimedium 'Pink Elf', one of the best of Robin White's hybrids.

The Future of Hybridizing

Many innovative nursery owners who stock varied epimediums have discovered seedlings growing in the cracks and crevices of their standing-beds and bulked up the little plants to sell to keen customers. Elizabeth Strangman discovered *Epimedium* 'Enchantress' in just such a manner in the 1990s, and it still holds its head up high in good company.

The wider distribution of these excellent hybrids awakened the imaginations of some of Europe and America's leading specialist growers, and more recently among ground-breaking nursery owners in Australia. These new hybrids, with excellent evergreen foliage and dramatically coloured flowers in all forms, offer so much to gardeners in all parts of the temperate world. There is enormous potential for creating some exceptional plants from the liaisons of species brought together for the first time in one nursery.

Some enterprising nursery owners are very excited by the astounding plants that arise from deliberate crossing and by chance. They are selecting plants for the size of the

Foliage of *Epimedium* ×*versicolor* 'Sulphureum' can tolerate frost, turning from green to bronze in winter.

Epimedium 'Enchantress', one of the loveliest bicoloured forms, was discovered in a garden in the 1990s.

flowers, their ability to hold the blooms well above the foliage, and the colours of the new leaves in contrast to the flowers. Others are concentrating on the habit of the plants, particularly their ability to grow and spread in dry shade and still carry big, beautiful blossoms. The results are just beginning to appear on the market, like the first splashes of a tidal wave breaking on the shore.

Other epimediums are content to flower off and on until mid-summer, a trait that some breeders are encouraging. Many, but by no means all, epimediums are evergreen, and a new debate has arisen over whether it is judicious to cut off over-wintered foliage before a plant flowers. Again, many breeders are looking for the ability of a plant to flower well above the mound of foliage, leaving the gardener merely to tidy up any damaged leaves just before flowering.

Late spring frosts are another factor that may cause the new flowers to burn, and one that breeders are aiming to obviate. They are selecting for later-flowering hybrids that do not put their heads up over their leaves until the frosts have passed, which is another reason to refrain from cutting back over-wintered leaves. A realistic alternative in the garden would be to plant them beneath overhanging evergreen shrubs and trees to provide just a little frost protection.

EUROPE

As the potential for breeding and introducing new hybrids of Chinese epimediums makes an impact on European nurseries, many growers are taking on the challenge. Some nursery owners are investigating the potential for creating hybrids between species from different parts of the world. The aim is to produce epimediums that have all the attributes of the Chinese species but mirror the vigour and dry-shade tolerance of traditional epimediums (such as *Epimedium pinnatum* and its subspecies).

In the United Kingdom the Chinese species and hybrids are proving popular as they are especially well adapted to the changing weather, when increasingly often there are periods of drought followed by long weeks of rain. Temperatures can now fluctuate alarmingly for the weather-sensitive British, who are used to a pattern of four sunny days and a thunderstorm in summer, and four freezing days and a heat wave in winter. Many growers are aiming to develop a race of epimediums with big, dramatic flowers and good foliage that can weather dry shade.

France—Thierry Delabroye. One of the most exciting nurseries in Europe is Pépinières Delabroye at Hantay, which is south of Lille in northern France. Since about 2006, owner Thierry Delabroye has turned his attention to breeding and selecting epimediums. And what epimediums they are.

Ever seeking the new, the improved, and the better, Delabroye selects plants primarily for their foliage, the height of the flower spikes above the leaves, and the colour contrast of the flowers, petals, and sepals with the leaves. He especially likes big flowers, claws, and spiders. Following a series of very cold springs, he is also selecting for plants that flower after the late spring frosts are over. He grows his selections on in raised beds around the nursery, testing them for their tolerance of the sometimes extreme weather in his area.

Delabroye has already launched a series, Magique Elfes, that comprises seedlings from the best of his breeding. He has also named many plants that will soon be making a splash more widely in Europe and in the United States. Varieties such as *Epimedium* 'Space Wagon', *E.* 'Lastalaica', and *E.* 'Ambrosine' are outstanding.

All of Delabroye's selections are the result of several generations of breeding. He grows the parent plants in a shade tunnel screened at the doors with netting to prevent bees from corrupting his work. Over the years he has found that it is difficult to make the first inter-specific cross—that is, to hybridize between two different species. But once the seedlings of that cross have appeared, he finds that they hybridize between each other more readily. Delabroye does the pollination in the evenings, in the dark, while wearing a light on his head. He is a man on a mission. When I visited him, sitting on his workbench was an epimedium with a distinct scent. In true Gallic style, he had picked it out with his nose.

Belgium—Koen Van Poucke. Tucked behind a row of shops in Heistraat, just over the border into Belgium, lies Koen Van Poucke's nursery in Sint-Niklaas. Ostensibly it sells cut flowers and big, lovely plants for containers, but if you step further in, you will be greeted by row after row of some of the most beautiful epimediums imaginable. They are a testament to the owner's passion.

Van Poucke grew up in this old-fashioned herbaceous nursery, which his father ran for years but had to close when the son was 15 years old. But the younger Van Poucke was undeterred, and he studied landscaping and restarted the nursery eight years later, in 1984. His father had not stocked epimediums, but when Van Poucke encountered his first one in the private garden of famous Belgian landscaper Jacques Wirtz, he was smitten. He had always had an interest in new, charming plants, and he could see the commercial potential for epimediums.

Travelling to England to visit Elizabeth Strangman's collection, as well as Robin White's, Van Poucke bought specimens of all the new forms. When Stearn's monograph was published, interest in epimediums began to take off. Van Poucke purchased a selection of Darrell Probst's plants from the United States. Then he went to Japan and had the honour of meeting Mikinori Ogisu and visiting several small Japanese *Epimedium* nurseries. He recalls buying "wonderful new Japanese *Epimedium grandiflorum* varieties, which were a great improvement on the old stock from Von Siebold," and he brought to Europe a very special soft salmon-pink coloured form, *E. grandiflorum* 'Akagiza Kura'.

Belgium—Daniëlle Monbaliu. Daniëlle Monbaliu runs a small specialist nursery, Epimedium, in Oostkampe. She grows a selection of exceptional plants, but as the name of her nursery suggests, she specializes in epimediums. Monbaliu has roughly 125 different varieties, both species and named hybrids, and propagates for sale about 35 of these. She grows the stock plants in the ground to familiarize herself with their tolerances and

A seedling on Thierry Delabroye's workbench selected for further breeding.

ways, and she selects for sale the forms that she finds especially beautiful—those that flower over a long period, are hardy enough to withstand the cold temperatures of the plains of Flanders, and need little or no support.

Over the years Monbaliu has come across one or two especially remarkable epimediums, among them *Epimedium* 'Marco', a lovely red-flowered variety with leaves splashed with oxblood red. She says she spotted it as a seedling growing in the nursery of Marco van Noort and named it after him.

England—Julian Sutton. Julian Sutton of Desirable Plants in Devon has taken up the challenge of crossing species that grow thousands of miles apart and seeing what comes up. His enthusiasm for creating a plant that has good flowers and foliage, and performs well in dry shade, is beginning to produce results. He has succeeded in crossing *Epimedium latisepalum* with *E. pinnatum* subsp. *colchicum*, and his *E.* 'Totnes Turbo' is the first commercial trail-blazer. The plant inherits its bi-coloured flowers from the latter parent, but has more and taller flower stems of deeper coloured flowers that are sometimes branched.

Sutton made this (likely first) controlled cross of the two species using *Epimedium pinnatum* subsp. *colchicum* as the seed parent, producing a more compact plant than this parent. So far it has proven to be a good spreader, but he is still testing its drought tolerance. To give it a real challenge he has planted it at the foot of a high wall within 1 m (40 in.) of a mature beech. He says this "will sort the men from the boys." If the plant succeeds, it could prove to be the parent of a whole race of epimediums that grow well in dry shade. Every enthusiast and gardener will be waiting with bated breath for the next introduction.

Epimedium 'Totnes Turbo', bred by Julian Sutton.

England—Karan, Nick, and Torsten Junker. Also working in Devon are the Junkers. When Robin White decided to close Blackthorn Nursery, he looked around for someone he could trust to maintain and grow his collection. He chose Karan and Nick Junker, whose nursery at the time was on a site near Taunton in Somerset. It was quite limited in size, and the family decided to relocate further west to Milverton, West Somerset. This was a brave move. It has taken up to five years to clear 50 acres of ground and get the new nursery, the stock planting, and the extended garden up and running.

The Junkers have built polytunnels and shade houses and laid down paths, drives, and a car park—all the while watering plants daily in summer, protecting them from late frosts, and propagating them. Their house is still under development. The result so far is very exciting. Their new site has been planted with stock trees to provide grafting material for the nursery and shrubs for cuttings, and they are growing the entire collection of epimediums that White passed along.

Karan and Nick's son, Torsten, has started breeding and selecting a few special epimediums. His main goal in breeding new hybrids is to choose a good flower held above the leaves. The blossoms need not be very big, as he notes, "bigger is not always better and not everyone wants huge flowers." The shape is important, and colour contrast should be good. The flowers should last a long time and weather well. But also they should have good foliage, with interestingly shaped leaves that are well marked or colourful in spring and preferably autumn.

Like so many in the business, Torsten and his parents realize that there could be a profusion of similar hybrids, so he is prepared to name only those that are distinctly different, as he feels there are too many already to name for the sake of naming. He has so far selected *Epimedium* 'Autumn Raspberry' and *E.* 'Lemon Meringue Pie'. And *E.* 'Heavenly Purple' is a selection from *E.* 'Pink Constellation', as well as a winning play on words. There will no doubt be more on the way.

England—Keith Wiley. A third UK hybridizer in Devon is Keith Wiley of Wildside Nursery. He and his wife, Ros, have created a ground-breaking new garden. Wiley is another recipient of Robin White's hybrid epimediums, notably *Epimedium* 'Milky Way', *E.* 'Flowers of Sulphur', *E. acuminatum* 'Persian Carpet', *E.* 'Arctic Wings', and the excellent *E.* 'Honeybee'. Wiley continues to grow these in the garden at Wildside and sells them to his visitors.

From seedlings of these plants Wiley has also selected more lovely hybrids of his own. And they do broadcast their seedlings. He tests these to see if any is distinctly different from the existing forms. Whereas it would be tempting to name each and every new plant, he too recognizes that very soon the gardening world would be overwhelmed with named epimediums that are barely different from one another. Keith and Ros have named just five: *E.* 'Wildside Ruby', *E.* 'Buff Beauty', *E.* 'Buckland Spider', *E. grandiflorum* 'Wildside Red', and *E.* 'Wildside Amber', which Wiley says is a bit too similar to White's lovely *E.* 'Amber Queen'. All these plants contribute novelty, colour, and drama to the garden, in keeping with the tradition of Wildside Nursery.

Epimedium 'Wildside Ruby', bred by Keith Wiley.

AUSTRALIA

The gardeners of Australia are enthusiastic and keen to grow bright new epimediums. Enterprising nursery owners are just as excited to import them, bulk them up, and sell them to their customers. However, Australia is a notoriously difficult place to import any plant material that has health restrictions, but one or two nurseries with their own quarantine stations have brought in collections from the United States and Europe. More and more retail nurseries in Australia are making a specialty of epimediums.

Victoria—Matt Reed. At Antique Perennials in Kinglake, Matt Reed, who has been collecting epimediums for more than 12 years, runs a thriving wholesale nursery with 94 varieties of *Epimedium*. The nursery is situated in the hills outside Melbourne at 550 m (1800 ft.) elevation. Reed can grow most species and cultivars well—not only the old favourite ground-covering varieties, but many of the newer hybrids like *Epimedium* 'Pierre's Purple', *E. grandiflorum* 'Spring Wedding', and *E.* 'Spine Tingler'. Stock plants are grown in the ground, mostly in morning sun and then bright shade, and Reed finds that many are "too vigorous." These are divided every year in the stock beds.

The nursery grows all its plants in 13-cm (5-in.) pots for sale to retail nurseries and garden centres in the cooler areas of Australia around Melbourne, the Blue Mountains, the Southern Highlands in New South Wales, the hills around Adelaide, and even into Queensland. The epimediums are always in great demand, and they invariably sell out. Garden designers and landscapers are starting to understand how tough and valuable epimediums are for shaded positions, and how well they compete with tree roots and, in some cases, cope with dry shade. The nursery relies on reputation. It does not have an on-line presence, so good reports from influential designers are important.

Reed is starting to breed epimediums. Already he has produced an impressive hybrid of *Epimedium epsteinii* with huge lavender-purple flowers, much bigger than the norm. In the Australian winter he travels to North America and the United Kingdom in search of more lovely forms.

New South Wales—David Kennedy. Of all perennials, epimediums are David Kennedy's first love. To him they are like orchids, and the different forms, flowers, and leaf shapes captivate him. He has been importing them from Darrell Probst in the United States and from China, and has gathered a large collection of about 160 different species and cultivars at Clover Hill Rare Plants in Katoomba. He stocks one or two very rare species, such as *Epimedium trifoliatobinatum*, which he obtained from Probst. This species was originally collected in Shikoku, Japan, and has small spurred white-and-cream flowers over evergreen foliage.

Epimedium 'Spring Cascade', bred by David Kennedy.

Kennedy has found that epimediums grow well in the more temperate parts of Australia, such as Tasmania, South Australia, Victoria, and much of New South Wales (with the exception of the hot coastal areas). Some of the evergreen varieties do well in the northern suburbs of Sydney, but the deciduous types need cold winters to flower well.

Kennedy is also doing a lot of breeding using *Epimedium wushanense* spiny-leaved form crossed with *E. fargesii*. He has named one outstanding hybrid, *E.* 'Scary Fairies'. It is a strange pale yellow flower with horns. He is also working on crossing *E. fargesii* with *E. stellulatum*. One hybrid has stood out from the rest, and he has named it *E.* 'Spring Cascade'. He has also introduced *E.* 'Mardi Gras', a cross between *E. grandiflorum* 'White Queen' and *E.* ×*rubrum*. It has a clean bi-coloured flower: palest cream spurs held horizontally beneath small but strong pink sepals.

Tasmania—Sally Johannsohn. Of all parts of Australia, perhaps the island of Tasmania has the best climate for epimediums. Tasmanian gardeners are far from the scorching dry heat of central and eastern Australia. Here Sally Johannsohn runs Plant Hunters, a small specialist nursery in the cool climate of the foothills of Mount Wellington in Neika. The island's rich basalt soils grow a wide range of perennial hardy plants well, most especially epimediums.

Johannsohn has collected unusual perennials from Asia, North America's woodlands, and Europe for more than 20 years. Her first *Epimedium* acquisition was a little plant of *Epimedium* ×*youngianum* 'Niveum', which she chose for its foliage as well as its white flowers. She has always been attracted to foliage plants ever since she trained as a florist at the Constance Spry School in London in 1977. Here she was introduced to all sorts of foliage textures and colours, so when she started gardening she would go to great lengths to find those interesting foliage plants that she had encountered at the school and in the English gardens she visited. And "of course," she says, "I love the secretive, starry flowers on wiry stems."

Johannsohn imports plants from the better-known nurseries in the United States and Europe, and exchanges plants and seed with local collectors. She grows the original imported plants and some of their progeny mostly in pots in her garden and nursery. She does not breed new forms deliberately, but occasionally pots up a seedling. To date none has been named.

Beautiful *Epimedium* 'Mardi Gras'.

Epimedium ×*youngianum* 'Niveum' bears entirely white flowers with more open sepals that stand up and away from the petals, as well as tiny white spurs.

She does almost all of her own propagation and grows on the young plants on site, so she has detailed knowledge about which plants, including epimediums, work in different situations. Her list of epimediums for sale is long and varied, including *Epimedium pinnatum* subsp. *colchicum* 'Thunderbolt', with its striking chocolate brown and green evergreen foliage that makes dense clumps in dry shade. She also finds that it can cope with the more open situation in Tasmania better than in many other parts of Australia.

UNITED STATES

As mentioned previously, Darrell Probst has been a key player in the American introduction of many new species from China. He has gone on to hybridize and select some of the most inspired, and inspiring, forms in the world of epimediums. His hybrids have been taken up and added to by Tony Avent of Plant Delights Nursery and the Juniper Level Botanic Garden, while the nursery Probst started continues under the scrutiny of Karen Perkins.

The dramatic foliage of *Epimedium pinnatum* subsp. *colchicum* 'Thunderbolt' growing in Sally Johannsohn's garden in Neika, Tasmania.

Epimedium acuminatum 'Night Mistress' adds colour in a woodland planting that also includes variegated *Arum* and white-flowered bloodroot (*Sanguinaria canadensis* 'Flore Pleno').

Massachusetts—Karen Perkins. Karen Perkins now runs Garden Vision Epimediums in Phillipston, where she sells Darrell Probst's hybrids and wild-collected species and their selections. She has been working with Probst since he started the nursery, and with his collection of epimediums since 2001.

There are so many hybrids from which to choose that it is invidious to select one or two. From his collection of *Epimedium acuminatum* in 2000, Probst selected and named the wonderful *E. acuminatum* 'Night Mistress', with long pink spurs over dark purple petals that are suspended over the new foliage. He has also bred other exceptional hybrids, such as *E.* 'Domino', which produces clouds of white-and-maroon flowers on tall 60-cm (24-in.) stems over well-marked foliage, and *E.* 'Pink Champagne', with two-tone pink flowers over mounds of evergreen foliage speckled with purple.

North Carolina—Tony Avent. Tony Avent is the owner of Plant Delights Nursery, the mail-order nursery division of Juniper Level Botanic Garden in Raleigh. He established the business in 1988 to research and conserve rare plants, and to propagate, develop, and introduce others that are new to commerce in the United States.

Avent supports the introduction of some exceptional new epimediums. He introduces a few every year based on certain criteria. The most important is that the plant should be quite distinct from previous introductions. Other factors include that the flowers should be large, plentiful, and held well above the foliage, which itself should have really good colour. He selects for vigour in the garden and length of flowering. His introductions are good examples of these qualities.

Epimedium 'Chocolatte', bred by Tony Avent.

In a specific area alongside other existing species and cultivars, Avent trials open-pollinated seedlings. This placement allows him to compare seedlings with potential against current standards. After selecting the very best new seedlings, the nursery builds up numbers within four to six years, depending on their vigour. Avent then plants some into the public display gardens, and the remainder he puts up for sale to mail-order customers.

Among the many hybrids Avent has developed are one or two must-haves for any enthusiast. *Epimedium* 'Chocolatte' is an *E.* ×*omeiense* selection with white-spurred petals and sepals that fade to the eponymous soft brown at the centre. *Epimedium* 'Candy Striper' has very different flowers that comprise four white petals without spurs, but with distinct dark pink central stripes and purple-edged leaves that set off the flowers. Then there's *E.* 'Razzleberry', with sharp white sepals covering large purple petals with a golden margin to the mouth. And there are many others.

NON-COMMERCIAL GROWERS AND ENTHUSIASTS

In addition to the nursery owners who breed and hybridize epimediums, there are several non-commercial growers and enthusiasts.

United States—Richard Lighty. Richard Lighty has been fascinated by plants since the age of 10, and he has spent a long life researching plant genetics. He visited Korea in the mid-1960s and travelled for four months, collecting cuttings, live plants, and seeds that he shipped home. Despite the gruelling conditions, he notes, he "never lost a thing."

Lighty and his wife, Sally, gardened at Springwood, Kennett Square in Pennsylvania for many years. It was a garden of 7.5 acres, rich in acid soil and the moist but draining structure that epimediums and many other woodland plants require. Lighty grew nearly 50 epimediums in both light shade and full sun. Many of his plants were related to Japanese *Epimedium grandiflorum*. He found the only problem with the more open areas in full sun was that the evergreen epimediums sometimes suffered from winter burn.

An avid gardener, Lighty was fascinated by the variability of seedlings. He grew many self-sown seedlings in his collection and watched them for several years before naming one of them *Epimedium* 'Alabaster'. It is clump forming, long lasting, and vigorous without being invasive. Lighty believes it is a cross between *E. diphyllum* and *E.* ×*youngianum* 'Niveum', although it does not appear to have inherited a preference for acid soil like the latter parent.

England—Colin Crosbie. Colin Crosbie is curator of the Royal Horticultural Society Garden Wisley, in Surrey and an enthusiastic private collector as well. The Wisley garden has an interesting collection of older cultivars, some of which are unique examples of nineteenth- and early-twentieth-century species. Crosbie lives in a house on site that includes a large garden, and though he is an all-around plant enthusiast, he is particularly fond of plants for shade and of epimediums. Over the years, he has gathered quite a collection, which he planted in the acid green sands of his garden, and slowly this element is coming together.

In his rare moments away from the RHS garden, Crosbie is clearing the undergrowth and planting all manner of rare shade-lovers among his own *Epimedium* collection. His professional contact with some of the most interesting nursery owners in Europe has meant that he has often had the opportunity to buy epimediums that have barely hit the commercial nurseries. A walk around his garden in spring is a rare treat.

England—Roger Hammond. Roger Hammond holds the British National Collection of Epimediums at The Magnolias in Brentwood, Essex. Plant Heritage, formerly known as the National Council for the Conservation of Plants and Gardens, is a British organization that conserves the entirety of a given genus in the hands of one or two enthusiasts. It supports those whom it nominates as National Collection holders. Each collection must comprise at least three of every species and cultivar, including one grown in a container, and have a comprehensive catalogue and records.

Hammond has been enthusiastically collecting and growing epimediums since the late 1960s, when he first came across the expansive spreading forms and made a collection of the few that were available then. He found that these older plants were among the most weed-suppressing examples of any low ground-cover plants available. Even thugs such as horsetails (*Equisetum*) seemed hardly able to penetrate the tight mat of rhizomes of, say, *Epimedium* ×*warleyense*.

Epimedium 'Path Finder' growing on the corner of a path in Roger Hammond's garden.

In the late 1990s, Hammond attended an RHS Flower Show in Westminster, where he found Robin White's newly imported Chinese species to be mind blowing. He bought several then, and others at subsequent shows. He was smitten and a collection was born. Many of his plants are still thriving in his garden. Some have never been disturbed. Some have been lost. These he puts down mostly to their over-enthusiastic neighbours. He blames some casualties on slugs that ate off all the new growth as it appeared in spring, and a few to the occasional summer of severe drought.

Hammond gardens on good Essex loam over London clay in much of the garden. This means the soil can remain moist for longer than the Essex location might suggest. The pH is around neutral. He gives the plants a 5-cm (2-in.) mulch of year-old leaf mould each autumn, as recommended by William Stearn, and he waters them during a drought, mostly by watering can, from the ponds in the garden.

Hammond already has more than 200 different species, varieties, and hybrids, and has added over 160 new plants. And, like all real enthusiasts, he continues to collect. He named a chance seedling *Epimedium* 'Path Finder' because he found it by the path. It starts flowering quite late, and in its second year of flowering it continued into early September. Its seed parent was *E. membranaceum* and a good guess at the pollen parent would be *E. wushanense* 'Caramel', which has a touch of orange in the flower.

WHERE TO BUY

AUSTRALIA

Antique Perennials
P.O. Box 30
Kinglake, Victoria 3763

Clover Hill Rare Plants
P.O. Box 603
Katoomba 2789, N.S.W.
www.cloverhillrareplants.com

Plant Hunters
1115 Huon Road
Neika, Tasmania TAS 7054
www.planthunters.com.au

BELGIUM

Epimedium
Meulestee 56
8020 Oostkamp
www.epimedium.be

Koen Van Poucke
Heistraat 106
9100, Sint-Niklaas
www.koenvanpoucke.be

CANADA

Free Spirit Nursery
20405 32 Avenue
Langley, British Columbia V2Z 2C7
www.freespiritnursery.ca

Mason House Gardens
3520 Durham Road #1, RR #4
Uxbridge, Ontario L9P 1R4
www.masonhousegardens.com

Thimble Farms Nursery
175 Arbutus Road
Salt Spring Island
British Columbia V8K 1A3
www.thimblefarms.com

FRANCE

Pépinières Delabroye
Rue Roger Salengro 40
Hantay 59496
www.mytho-fleurs.com/les_vivaces_de_sandrine_et_thierry.htm

UNITED KINGDOM

Cotswold Garden Flowers
Sands Lane
Badsey
Evesham, Worcestershire
England WR11 7EZ
www.cgf.net

Desirable Plants
Pentamar
Crosspark
Totnes, Devon
England TQ9 5BQ
www.desirableplants.com
Mail order only.

Edrom Nurseries
Coldingham
Eyemouth
Berwickshire
Scotland TD14 5TZ
www.edrom-nurseries.co.uk

Junker's Nursery
Higher Cobhay
Milverton, Somerset
England TA4 1NJ
www.junker.co.uk
By appointment.

Long Acre Plants
Charlton Musgrove
Near Wincanton, Somerset
England BA9 8EX
www.plantsforshade.co.uk

Mill Cottage Plants
Henley Mill
Wookey, Somerset
England BA5 1AW
www.millcottageplants.co.uk

UNITED STATES

Arrowhead Alpines
1310 North Gregory Road
P.O. Box 857
Fowlerville, Michigan 48836
www.arrowheadalpines.com

Collector's Nursery
16804 NE 102nd Avenue
Battle Ground, Washington 98604
www.collectorsnursery.com

Fairweather Gardens
P.O. Box 330
Greenwich, New Jersey 08323
www.fairweathergardens.com

Garden Vision Epimediums
P.O. Box 50
Templeton, Massachusetts 01468
www.epimediums.com

Lazy S'S Farm
2360 Spotswood Trail
Barboursvills, Virginia 22923
www.lazyssfarm.com

Plant Delights Nursery
9241 Sauls Road
Raleigh, North Carolina 27603
www.plantdelights.com

WHERE TO SEE

BELGIUM

Ghent University Botanic Garden
Plantentuin Universiteit Gent
K.L. Ledeganckstraat 35
Ghent B-9000
www.plantentuin.ugent.be

CANADA

University of British Columbia Botanical Garden
6804 SW Marine Drive
Vancouver, British Columbia V6T 1Z4
www.botanicalgarden.ubc.ca

UNITED KINGDOM

Edrom Nurseries
Coldingham
Eyemouth
Berwickshire TD14 5TZ
Scotland
www.edrom-nurseries.co.uk
Has a newly planted 4-acre garden of epimediums and shade-loving perennials

The Garden House at Buckland Monachorum
Yelverton
Devon
England PL20 7LQ
www.thegardenhouse.org.uk

Cherubeer Gardens
Higher Cherubeer
Dolton
Devon
England EX19 8PP
Open under the National Gardens Scheme

Junker's Nursery
Higher Cobhay
Milverton
Somerset
England TA4 1NJ
www.junker.co.uk
Karan, Nick, and Torsten Junker have been planting up their newly acquired 50 acres with trees, shrubs, and perennials. They include Robin White's collection and others, including those bred by Torsten.

National Collection of Epimediums
The Magnolias
Brentwood, Essex
England
www.themagnolias.co.uk
A private garden. Roger Hammond's collection is available to see by appointment only.

Royal Botanic Gardens, Kew
Richmond
Surrey
England TW9 3AB
www.kew.org
William Stearn's collection of epimediums at the Woodland Garden at Kew is planted at the base of the mound by the Temple of Aeolus. Map ref N7.

Marwood Hill Gardens
Marwood
Barnstaple
North Devon
England EX31 4EB
www.marwoodhillgarden.co.uk
The gardens are always changing and lately include a collection of epimediums.

Royal Horticultural Society Garden
Wisley
Woking
Surrey
England GU23 6QB
www.rhs.org.uk/Gardens/Wisley
A collection of the classic spreading forms of epimediums.

Savill Garden
Windsor Great Park
Windsor
England SL4 2HT
www.thecrownestate.co.uk
Head Gardener Harvey Stephens worked with William Stearn as a student and has planted a number of new Chinese epimediums in the woodland gardens.

Wildside Nursery
Green Lane
Buckland Monachorum
Yelverton
Devon
England PL20 7NP
www.wileyatwildside.com
Keith and Ros Wiley have created a remarkable garden.

UNITED STATES

Bloedel Reserve
7571 NE Dolphin Drive
Bainbridge Island, Washington 98110
www.bloedelreserve.org

The Botanic Garden at Smith College
College Lane
Northampton, Massachusetts 01063
www.smith.edu/gardens

Chanticleer
786 Church Road
Wayne, Pennsylvania 19087
www.chanticleergarden.org

Coastal Maine Botanical Gardens
132 Botanical Gardens Drive (off Barters Island Road)
Boothbay, Maine 04537
www.mainegardens.org

Elisabeth C. Miller Botanical Garden
P.O. Box 77377
Seattle, Washington 98177
www.millergarden.org

Juniper Level Botanic Gardens
9241 Sauls Road
Raleigh, North Carolina 27603
www.juniperlevelbotanicgarden.org

New York Botanical Garden
2900 Southern Boulevard
Bronx, NY 10458
www.nybg.org

Sarah P. Duke Gardens
420 Anderson Street, Duke University
Durham, North Carolina 27708
www.gardens.duke.edu

U.S. National Arboretum Asian Collections
3501 New York Avenue, NE
Washington, DC 20002
www.usna.usda.gov

Wave Hill
675 West 252nd Street
Bronx, New York 10471
www.wavehill.org

FOR MORE INFORMATION

BOOKS

Barker, David G. 1998. *Epimediums and Other Herbaceous Berberidaceae*. Worcestershire, England: The Hardy Plant Society.

Hinkley, Daniel J. 1999. *The Explorer's Garden: Rare and Unusual Perennials*. Portland, Oregon: Timber Press.

Levy, Ran. 1995. *The Flora of Japan*. Tokyo, Japan: Kodansha International.

Phillips, Roger, and Martyn Rix. 1991. *Perennials*. Vol. 1, Early Perennials. London, England: Pan Books.

Stearn, William T. 2002. *The Genus Epimedium and Other Herbaceous Berberidacea, including the Genus Podophyllum*. London, England: The Board of Trustees of the Royal Botanic Gardens, Kew.

Wiley, Keith. 2006. *Shade: Planting Solutions for Shady Gardens*. London, England: Mitchell Beazley.

Woodward, Marcus. 1985. *Gerard's Herball: The Essence thereof from the Edition of Th. Johnson 1636*. London, England: Bracken Books.

WEBSITES

Canadian Gardening: www.canadiangardening.com

Chicago Botanic Garden: www.chicagobotanic.org

Darrell Probst: www.home.earthlink.net/~darrellpro. Photos of Darrell's epimediums

Flora of China: www.efloras.org. Vol. 19 has *Epimedium*.

John Jearrard's Herbal: www.johnjearrard.co.uk/plants/epimedium. Managed by an epimedium expert and enthusiast.

Missouri Botanical Garden: www.missouribotanicalgarden.org

Northwest Horticultural Society: www.northwesthort.org/garden_notes_pdf/gn_spring_2011.pdf

RHS Wisley: www.rhs.org.uk. Details of the British National Plant Collection held at Wisley in Surrey, England

University of Vermont: pss.uvm.edu/pss123/perepmid.html

ORGANIZATIONS

Alpine Garden Society: www.alpinegardensociety.net

Hardy Plant Society: www.hardy-plant.org.uk

Hardy Plant Society/Mid-Atlantic Group: www.hardyplant.org

Hardy Plant Society of Oregon: www.hardyplantsociety.org

Ontario Rock Garden and Hardy Plant Society: www.onrockgarden.com

Plant Heritage: www.nccpg.com

Salem Hardy Plant Society: www.salemhardyplantsociety.org

Scottish Rock Garden Club: www.srgc.net

Vancouver Hardy Plant Group: www.vancouverhardyplant.org

Wisconsin Hardy Plant Society: www.wisconsinhardyplantsociety.com

HARDINESS ZONE TEMPERATURES

USDA ZONES & CORRESPONDING TEMPERATURES

Temp °F			Zone	Temp °C		
-60	to	-55	1a	-51	to	-48
-55	to	-50	1b	-48	to	-46
-50	to	-45	2a	-46	to	-43
-45	to	-40	2b	-43	to	-40
-40	to	-35	3a	-40	to	-37
-35	to	-30	3b	-37	to	-34
-30	to	-25	4a	-34	to	-32
-25	to	-20	4b	-32	to	-29
-20	to	-15	5a	-29	to	-26
-15	to	-10	5b	-26	to	-23
-10	to	-5	6a	-23	to	-21
-5	to	0	6b	-21	to	-18
0	to	5	7a	-18	to	-15
5	to	10	7b	-15	to	-12
10	to	15	8a	-12	to	-9
15	to	20	8b	-9	to	-7
20	to	25	9a	-7	to	-4
25	to	30	9b	-4	to	-1
30	to	35	10a	-1	to	2
35	to	40	10b	2	to	4
40	to	45	11a	4	to	7
45	to	50	11b	7	to	10
50	to	55	12a	10	to	13
55	to	60	12b	13	to	16
60	to	65	13a	16	to	18
65	to	70	13b	18	to	21

FIND HARDINESS MAPS ON THE INTERNET.
United States *http://www.usna.usda.gov/Hardzone/ushzmap.html*
Canada *http://www.planthardiness.gc.ca/*
Europe *http://www.gardenweb.com/zones/europe/* or *http://www.uk.gardenweb.com/forums/zones/hze.html*

ACKNOWLEDGEMENTS

I would like to thank the very many people who have been so helpful to me on my long and tortuous journey into the world of epimediums. Those who have been especially supportive include Karen Perkins, who checked assiduously through my lists; Bob Brown, who took me to meet his French and Belgian contacts, including Thierry and Sandrine Delabroye, Daniëlle Monbaliu, and Koen Van Poucke, all of whom gave up their valuable time during a busy season; and Ro FitzGerald, who not only did the initial proof-reading but also introduced me to legendary gardener Joan Lorraine.

Thanks also to Darrell Probst and Roy Lancaster for their input on plant-collecting and nomenclature; Roger Hammond, Plant Heritage National Collection holder, for answering emails and providing images; Colin Crosbie and Billy McCutcheon of the RHS Garden, Wisley; Marc Libert, Ghent University Botanic Garden; Keith Wiley, Wildside Nursery; Nick Howarth, The Garden House at Buckland Monachorum; Malcolm Pharoah, Marwood Hill Gardens; Julian Sutton, Desirable Plants; Karan, Nick, and Torsten Junker, Junker's Nursery; Terry Hunt and Cath Davis, Edrom Nurseries; Tony Avent, Plant Delights Nursery; Matt Reed, Antique Perennials; David Kennedy, Clover Hill Rare Plants; and Sally Johannsohn, Plant Hunters. Many of these provided photographs for this book.

Thanks to Carol Clements and Jo Hynes for showing me their gardens; David Barker, Richard Lighty, Robin White, Mike and Sue Perkins, and Dan Pearson for their input; Mark Bolton for his lovely photographs of my own collection. Additional thanks for their photographs go to Gerard Van Buiten of the Hortulanus Botanische Tuinen Universitet, Utrecht; Bernard Dollet; Andrew Duncan; John Sirkett, aka John Jearrard; and Richie Steffen, Elizabeth C. Miller Botanical Garden.

Thanks to Anna Mumford and Linda Willms of Timber Press, as well as Sarah Rutledge Gorman, for their practical help and sound advice.

And, last but not least, thanks to my husband, Peter, for supporting my antisocial endeavours throughout this odyssey.

PHOTO CREDITS

Drawings are by **MARJORIE LEGGITT**.
Photographs are by the author except for the following:

COVER: (front) Andrea Jones; (spine) Mark Bolton/GAP; (back top row) Tony Avent; (back bottom right) Karen Perkins.

TONY AVENT, pages 66, 68, 97, 125 right, 140–141 center, 150, 172–173, and 219 right.
RICHARD BLOOM/GAP, page 14 right, design by Catherine Heatherington.
MARK BOLTON, pages 10, 54, 162, 182 lower, 185, and 205.
MARK BOLTON/GAP, pages 17 lower right and 210 left and right.
CHRIS BURROWS/GAP, page 217 lower.
THIERRY DELABROYE, page 189.
BERNARD DOLLET, pages 58 and 69.
ANDREW DUNCAN, pages 216 and 217 upper.
JOHN FISHER, OHIO DEPARTMENT OF AGRICULTURE, BUGWOOD.ORG, page 195.
SUZIE GIBBONS/GAP, page 40, design by Nigel Dunnett and The Landscape Agency; RBC New Wild Garden.
ROGER HAMMOND, pages 5 left & right, 7, 16, 48, 49, 51, 53, 55, 62, 65, 67, 71, 77, 78, 79, 83, 84 top, 90, 96, 101, 102, 106, 108, 115, 118, 120, 123, 124, 127, 128, 130, 134, 136, 138, 139, 145, 146, 153, 160 bottom, 161, 169, 176–177 center, 213, and 221.
STEPHEN HAUSER/BOTANIKFOTO, page 33 left.
SAXON HOLT, pages 34 and 199.
TERRY HUNT, pages 84 bottom, 87, 104, and 166.
SALLY JOHANNSOHN, pages 133 and 218–219 center.
ANDREA JONES/GARDEN EXPOSURES PHOTO LIBRARY, pages 25 left and 37.
LYNN KEDDIE/GAP, pages 36 and 179.
ROY LANCASTER, pages 6, 200, and 208 left.
MARC LIBERT, page 202.
MARTIN MULCHINOCK, page 238.
KAREN PERKINS, pages 61, 151 right, and 155.
HOWARD RICE/GAP, page 201 right.
JOHN SIRKETT, page 99.
RICHIE STEFFEN, pages 2–3, 26–27 top center, 89, 163 right, and 196–197.
GERARD VAN BUITEN, page 203.
KOEN VAN POUCKE, page 94.
KEITH WILEY, pages 214–215.

INDEX

Acer, 37, 175
Acer pensylvanicum, 41
Achlys, 198
acid soils, 36–39, 179, 184
aconite foliage, 12
Aconitum napellus, 30, 31
Acorus gramineus 'Ogon', 185
Alchemilla mollis, 33
Algeria, 128, 198, 200
alkaline soils, 30, 63, 179, 184
alpine epimedium, 33
Amelanchier, 175
Amelanchier laevis, 41
American cowslip, 17
Anemonella thalictroides f. rosea 'Oscar Schoaf', 19
Anemone nemerosa, 32
Anemone sylvestris, 41
annual honesty, 34
Antique Perennials, 216
Aquilegia, 42
Arbutus unedo, 37
Arum, 218
asparagus family (Asparagaceae), 185
Asplenium, 185
Asplenium scolopendrium, 36
  'Angustatum', 36
  Cristatum Group, 36
Astilbe 'Deutschland', 25
Athyrium niponicum var. *pictum*, 42
Athyrium otophorum var. *okanum*, 42
Aucuba japonica, 32
Australia, 216–218
Avent, Tony, 125, 189, 206, 218, 219–220
  hybrids of, 68, 97, 219, 220
azaleas, 37, 39

barberry, 198

barrenwort, 200
Beesia calthifolia, 30
Beijing Botanic Garden, 77
Belgium, 212–213
Berberis, 198
Bergenia, 9
Bergenia 'Overture', 26
Betula, 175
Betula ermanii, 40
Betula pendula, 40
Betula utilis var. *jacquemontii*, 40
birch, 40, 175
birch bark cherry, 41
black grass, 185
Blackthorn Nursery, 8, 55, 209, 214
bleeding hearts, 29
bloodroot, 42, 199
bluebells, 32–33, 176
Bodinier, Émile-Marie, 118
Bongardia, 198
Bowles' golden grass, 33, 185
breeders, 29, 56
brunnera, 39
Brunnera macrophylla, 33
  'Jack Frost', 34
  'Mr Morse', 34
Buckland Monachorum, 38
"Buddha Light," 9

calcicole species, 184
camellias, 37, 39
canopy, 40–41
Carex buchananii, 185
Carex conica 'Snowline', 185
Carex flagellifera, 185
Catherine the Great, Empress of Russia, 200
Caulophyllum, 198
Cercidiphyllum japonicum, 41, 175

Cercis siliquastrum, 41
Chanticleer Garden, 25
Chappell, Peter, 22, 110, 146
Chatto, Beth, 24
Chen Yi, 202
cherry, 40–41
chickweed, 195
Chilean fire bush, 37
China, 198, 200
Chinese birches, 40
Chinese epimediums, 7, 22, 38, 39–45, 205–208, 209, 211
  cultivation of, 9, 39–45, 179, 182
  flower size of, 19
  foliage of, 27, 29
  new species of, 48, 62, 65, 67, 71, 74, 77, 78, 79, 109, 115, 123, 160, 171
  older species of, 70, 118, 120, 134
Christmas box, 32
classification of epimediums, 204–205
clematis, 176
Clements, Carol, 30, 31
Clover Hill Rare Plants, 216
clumping epimediums, 34
Colchian barrenwort, 132
columbines, 42
companion plants, 9, 19, 29–45, 33–37, 184–186
compost, 177, 184
conifers, 175
conservation issues, 200–201
Constance Spry School, 217
Constantine mountains, 198, 200
containers, 182–187
Convallaria majalis 'Golden Jubilee', 32
coral bells, 14

Cornus alba 'Sibirica', 26
corydalis, 39, 40, 42
Corydalis flexuosa, 9, 42
Corydalis solida, 9
crab apples, 41, 175
Crataegus, 175
creeping navelwort, 34
Crosbie, Colin, 178, 220–221
cyclamen, 17

David, Armand, 70
deciduous woodlands, 31
deer, 193
Deinanthe bifida, 44
Deinanthe caerulea, 44
Delabroye, Thierry, 150, 189, 211–212
    hybrids of, 56, 58, 69, 72, 75, 114, 121, 144, 212
Desirable Plants, 213
Dicentra, 29
Dicentra formosa, 9
Dicentra 'Stuart Boothman', 30
Digitalis ferruginea, 14
Dioscorides, 199, 200
Diphylleia, 198
diseases, 191
Disporum sessile 'Variegatum', 25, 30, 31
division, 190–191
Dodecatheon meadia, 17
Dodson, Kelly, 149
dog's tooth violets, 37
dogwood(s), 9, 26
Doncaster, Amy, 166
Donkelaar, Andre, 153
drought-tolerant species, 33–36
Dryopteris affinis 'Crispa Gracilis', 185
dry shade, 12, 14, 24, 31–33, 200
    epimediums for, 127, 128, 134, 137, 152, 156
dwarf comfrey, 33

eared lady fern, 42
early cultivation of epimediums, 199–200

Elisabeth C. Miller Botanical Garden, 37
Embothrium coccineum, 37
Emei Shan (Mount Omei), 9, 22, 48, 49, 78, 124, 125, 188
England, 213–214, 220–221
Epimedium, origin of name, 199
Epimedium acuminatum, 13, 21, 48, 50, 176, 209, 219
    'Galaxy', 49, 206
    hybrids of, 54, 111, 124, 129, 187
    'Night Mistress', 21, 42, 50–51, 218, 219
    'Persian Carpet', 185, 214
Epimedium 'Akebono', 36, 52
Epimedium 'Alabaster', 18, 53, 220
Epimedium alpinum, 33, 137, 138, 156, 198, 199
Epimedium 'Amanogawa', 19, 20, 48, 54
Epimedium 'Amber Queen', 22, 35, 55, 175, 209, 214
Epimedium 'Ambrosine', 56, 212
Epimedium 'Arctic Wings', 20, 57, 209, 214
Epimedium 'Artanis', 58, 189
Epimedium 'Asiatic Hybrid', 33
Epimedium 'Autumn Raspberry', 214
Epimedium 'Black Sea', 15, 26, 59
Epimedium brachyrrhizum, 20, 26, 43, 60, 118
    'Elfin Magic', 20
    'Karen', 60, 61
Epimedium brevicornu, 15, 62
    var. *rotundatum*, 62
Epimedium 'Buckland Spider', 20, 63, 214
Epimedium 'Buff Beauty', 64, 214
Epimedium campanulatum, 15, 65
Epimedium 'Candy Striper', 66, 220

Epimedium 'Caramel', 161
Epimedium chlorandrum, 21, 67
Epimedium 'Chocolatte', 68, 219, 220
Epimedium 'Conalba', 53
Epimedium 'Cyrion', 69
Epimedium davidii, 15, 70, 81, 162
Epimedium 'Dawn', 52
Epimedium diphyllum, 15, 18, 53, 201, 220
Epimedium dolichostemon, 17, 48, 54, 71, 76, 79, 111, 187
Epimedium 'Domaine de St Jean de Beauregard', 72
Epimedium 'Domino', 73, 219
Epimedium ecalcaratum, 17, 65, 74, 116
Epimedium 'Egret', 21, 22, 75, 185
Epimedium 'Elf Orchid', 130
Epimedium 'Enchantress', 7–8, 21, 76, 210
Epimedium epsteinii, 21, 77, 216
Epimedium fangii, 48, 78, 124
Epimedium fargesii, 17, 67, 71, 79, 217
    'Pink Constellation', 80, 104
Epimedium 'Fire Dragon', 22, 23, 81, 209
Epimedium flavum, 55, 82
Epimedium 'Flowers of Sulphur', 82, 185, 188, 209, 214
Epimedium franchetii, 75, 83
    'Brimstone Butterfly', 8, 21, 83
Epimedium 'Fukujuji', 84
Epimedium 'Ghent Orange', 202
Epimedium 'Golden Eagle', 33, 34
Epimedium 'Golden Showers', 209
Epimedium grandiflorum, 9, 26, 36, 84, 85, 113, 179, 201, 212, 220

'Akagi Zakura', 86
'Akagiza Kura', 86, 212
'Beni Chidori', 87, 88
'Circe', 88
'Crimson Beauty', 104
'Crimson Queen', 104
'Dark Beauty', 27, 89
'Freya', 135
var. *higoense* 'Bandit', 26, 27, 90
var. *higoense* 'Confetti', 17, 18, 91
var. *higoense* 'Saturn', 92
hybrids of, 18–19, 63, 129, 137, 143, 153
'Kicho', 103
'Koji', 93
'Korin', 94
'La Rocaille', 95
'Lilafee', 7, 18, 96
'Pink Parasol', 97
'Purple Prince', 18, 98
'Queen Esta', 18, 99, 179
'Red Beauty', 104
'Red Queen', 104
'Rose Queen', 104
'Sirius', 18
'Spring Wedding', 100, 216
'Tama-no-genpei', 101
var. *violaceum*, 168
'White Queen', 18, 102, 217
'Wildside Red', 214
'Yellow Princess', 103
'Yubae', 88, 89, 104, 162
Epimedium 'Heavenly Purple', 13, 104–105, 214
Epimedium 'Hina Matsuri', 106
Epimedium 'Honeybee', 42, 107, 214
Epimedium hunanense, 83
Epimedium ilicifolium, 108–109
Epimedium 'Jean O'Neill', 22, 23, 110
Epimedium 'Kaguyahime', 48, 111, 182, 187
Epimedium 'King Prawn', 38, 39, 112

Epimedium 'Kodai Murasaki', 113
Epimedium koreanum, 63
Epimedium 'Lastalaica', 114, 212
Epimedium latisepalum, 57, 75, 112, 115, 213
Epimedium 'Lemon Meringue Pie', 214
Epimedium 'Lemon Zest', 116–117, 185
Epimedium leptorrhizum, 60, 76, 81, 118, 119, 131
'Mariko', 20, 119
Epimedium lishihchenii, 27, 120
Epimedium Magique Elfes Series, 121, 212
Epimedium 'Marco', 22, 23, 122, 213
Epimedium 'Mardi Gras', 217
Epimedium membranaceum, 19, 135, 158, 202, 221
subsp. *orientale*, 120
Epimedium mikinorii, 206
Epimedium 'Milky Way', 54, 214
Epimedium 'Mme Butterfly', 209
Epimedium nursery, 122
Epimedium ogisui, 8, 20, 30, 31, 57, 82, 115, 123, 205, 206
Epimedium ×*omeiense*, 48, 158, 220
'Akane', 8, 9, 13, 22, 124, 183, 185, 202
'Emei Shan', 8, 124
'Myriad Years', 125
'Razzleberry', 125, 126, 220
'Stormcloud', 22, 124, 126
Epimedium 'Path Finder', 221
Epimedium ×*perralchicum*, 127, 182
'Fröhnleiten, 7, 14, 24, 127, 128
Epimedium perralderianum, 128
Epimedium 'Persian Carpet', 185
Epimedium 'Phoenix', 21, 129

Epimedium 'Pierre's Purple', 216
Epimedium 'Pink Champagne', 20, 130, 219
Epimedium 'Pink Constellation', 214
Epimedium 'Pink Elf', 17, 131, 209
Epimedium pinnatum, 7, 128, 181, 211
subsp. *colchicum*, 9, 12, 14, 24, 59, 127, 132, 153, 156, 213
subsp. *colchicum* 'Thunderbolt', 133, 218
Epimedium platypetalum, 15, 65, 134
Epimedium pubescens, 6, 67, 131
Epimedium 'Red Maximum', 135
Epimedium rhizomatosum 'Golden Eagle', 136
Epimedium 'Rik', 202, 203, 204
Epimedium 'Roseum', 104
Epimedium ×*rubrum*, 15, 31, 32, 137, 176, 217
'Red Start', 138
'Sweetheart', 137, 138
Epimedium sagittatum, 200
'Warlord', 139
Epimedium 'Scary Fairies', 217
Epimedium sempervirens, 18, 36, 93, 137
'Candy Hearts', 18, 138, 140
'Mars', 18, 141
'Okuda's White', 18, 142
'Violet Queen', 18, 143
Epimedium 'Silver Queen', 89
Epimedium 'Space Wagon', 144, 212
Epimedium 'Spine Tingler', 145, 216
Epimedium 'Spinners', 22, 146
Epimedium 'Spinx Twinkler', 145
Epimedium 'Spring Cascade', 216, 217

Epimedium 'Star Cloud', 209
Epimedium stellulatum, 217
    'Wudang Star', 15, 16, 147, 206, 207, 209
    'Yukiko', 148
Epimedium 'Sunshowers', 149
Epimedium 'The Giant', 150, 208
Epimedium 'Totnes Turbo', 213
Epimedium trifoliatobinatum, 216
Epimedium ×*versicolor*, 24, 29, 30, 33, 36
    'Cherry Tart', 14, 151
    'Cupreum', 152, 153
    'Discolor', 152, 153, 154
    'Neosulphureum', 14, 15, 153, 154
    'Strawberry Blush', 153, 155
    'Sulphureum', 9, 24, 25, 153, 154, 178, 210
    'Versicolor', 153
Epimedium ×*warleyense*, 15, 33, 34, 156, 221
Epimedium 'Wildside Amber', 214
Epimedium 'Wildside Ruby', 26, 157, 214, 215
Epimedium 'William Stearn', 22, 23, 158, 185, 209
Epimedium 'Windfire', 158–159
Epimedium wushanense, 36, 112, 160, 161, 190, 206
    'Caramel', 8, 13, 22, 23, 55, 161, 208, 221
    Ogisu's form of, 28, 29, 160, 208
    spiny-leaved form, 160, 217
Epimedium 'Yōkihi', 162
Epimedium ×*youngianum*, 9, 18, 36, 52, 53
    'Azusa', 163
    'Be My Valentine', 164
    'Fairy Dust', 165
    'Merlin', 19, 53, 106, 166
    'Niveum', 167, 217, 220
    'Pink Star', 168
    'Purple Heart', 168

    'Tamabotan', 18, 19, 169
    'Yenomoto', 170
Epimedium zhushanense, 171
Epstein, Harold, 77, 89, 99
Epstein's epimedium, 77
Equisetum, 221
Eryngium 'Miss Willmott's Ghost', 156
Erythronium, 37
Erythronium dens-canis, 37
Erythronium 'Pagoda', 37
Erythronium revolutum, 37
Erythronium 'White Beauty', 37
eucryphias, 39
Euphorbia amygdaloides var. *robbiae*, 33
evergreen epimediums, 24, 29, 176, 181, 182, 211, 217, 220
evergreen grasses, 185

fairy bells, 25, 30
    variegated, 31
fall colour, 26
false bugbane, 30
Farges' epimedium, 79
Farges, Paul, 79
Far Reaches Farm, 149
Farrer, Reginald, 62
fencing, 193–194
ferns, 34, 36, 40, 42, 45
fertilizer, 39, 175, 184
flowers, 9, 13–23
foamflower, 34
foliage, 9, 24–29
Fortescue, Katherine and Lionel, 38–39
foxglove, 14
France, 211–212
frost, 42, 59, 182, 187, 211
    and leaf colour, 133, 210
    and seed germination, 190
frost protection, 131, 211

garden compost, 177
Garden House, 38–39
Garden Vision Epimediums, 62, 93, 219

Geranium 'Ann Folkard', 42
Geranium macrorrhizum
    'Bevan's Variety', 34
    'White-Ness', 34
Geranium phaeum 'Samobor', 29
Geranium 'Rozanne', 42
geraniums, 29, 34, 42
Geranium 'Sandrine', 42
Gerard, John, 199, 200
Ghent University Botanic Garden, 85, 137, 153, 201–202
Goetghebeur, Paul, 202
grasses, 33, 185
ground-covering plants, 14, 33, 38
ground layer, 41–45
growing, 182–187
Gymnospermium, 198

Hacquetia epipactis 'Thor', 30
Hamamelis ×*intermedia*, 37
    'Pallida', 37
Hammond, Roger, 221
hart's tongue, 36, 185
hawthorns, 175
heavenly bamboo, 198
heeling in, 180
hellebores, 26, 32, 43, 44, 204
Helleborus ×*hybridus*, 9, 32
herbaceous epimediums, 9, 24, 181, 190
herbal remedy, 200
Heuchera 'Ebony and Ivory', 14
heucheras, 29, 185
×*Heucherella*, 185
Higher Cherubeer, 38
Himalayan birches, 40
Himalayan blue poppy, 37
Himalayas, 41
Hinkley, Dan, 125, 206
holly-leaved epimedium, 109
Holt Farm, Somerset, England, 32
horny goat weed, 200
horsetails, 221
horticultural fleece, 187
hosta(s), 12, 29, 30

Hosta 'Great Expectations', 29
Hosta 'June', 29
Hughes, Kevin, 110
hybridization, 182
    in Australia, 216–218
    in Europe, 211–214
    in the United States, 218–220
    non-commercial, 220–221
hybrids, 29, 38, 39, 202, 209
Hydrangea aspera, 41
    'Mauvette', 41
    'Peter Chappell', 41
    'Villosa', 41
Hydrangea involucrata, 41
Hydrangea macrophylla, 41
    'Merveille Sanguine', 26
Hydrangea paniculata, 41
hydrangeas, 9, 41
Hydrangea serrata, 41
Hynes, Jo and Tom, 38

Ikariso, 85
iron absorption, 85, 177, 180

Japanese epimediums, 201–204
    for containers, 182, 184
    cultivation of, 42, 175, 179, 181
    species of, 18, 85, 216
Japanese ferns, 42
Japanese maple, 31, 175
Jeffersonia, 198, 199
Johannsohn, Sally, 217–218
Judas tree, 41
Juniper Level Botanic Garden, 218, 219
Junker, Karan and Nick, 214
Junker, Torsten, 104, 214
Junker's Nursery, 104, 214

katsura, 41, 175
Kawarda, 202
Keiga, Kawahar, 201
Kennedy, David, 216–217
Klose, Heinz, 127

labels, 184
lady's mantle, 33
Lancaster, Roy, 48, 49, 147, 204, 205, 206, 209
large-flowered barrenwort, 85
larger flowers, 19–23
leaf mould, 39, 174, 177–178, 191
    as mulch, 85, 118, 119, 221
leaf mould bins, 177, 178
leaves, 176, 186
Leontice, 198
Libert, Marc, 202, 204, 206, 208
Lighty, Richard, 53, 220
lily-of-the-valley, 32, 39
Linnaeus, Carl, 199
Liquidambar styraciflua, 37
Liriodendron tulipifera, 175
Li Shih-chen, 120
lists of epimediums
    acid-loving, 36
    clumping, 34
    for containers, 183
    evergreen, 24
    for fall foliage colour, 26
    herbaceous, 181
    large-flowered, 20
    small-flowered, 16
    spreading, 32
Lunaria annua, 34
Lunaria rediviva, 34
    'Partway White', 34
lungworts, 29, 42

magnolias, 39, 41
Magnolia sieboldii, 40, 41
Magnolia stellata, 41
Magnolias, The, 221
×*Mahoberberis*, 198
Mahonia, 198
Mahonia ×*media* 'Charity', 32
Maianthemum racemosum, 45
maintenance, 181–182
Malus, 41, 175
maple, 37
March, Skip, 133
Matteuccia struthiopteris, 25

Meconopsis baileyi, 37
Meconopsis punicea, 37
Medes, 199
medicinal uses, 200–201
medium-size flowers, 18–19
Milium effusum 'Aureum', 33, 185
Monbaliu, Daniëlle, 122, 212–213
monkshood, 30, 31
Mount Omei. *See* Emei Shan
mulch, 175, 176

Nandina, 198
National Collection of Epimediums, British, 221
National Council for the Conservation of Plants and Gardens, 221
Needham, Joseph, 120
nematodes, 193, 195
New South Wales, 216–217
non-commercial growers and enthusiasts, 220–221
North American Rock Garden Society, 77

Ogisu, Mikinori, 112, 118, 120, 212
    plant named for, 8, 20, 30, 31, 57, 82, 123, 205
    plants bred by, 28, 29
    plants collected by, 62, 67, 74, 79, 202, 205, 209
    plants discovered by, 65, 78, 205
    plants introduced by, 71, 109, 115, 206
    plants selected by, 48, 148, 160
Omphalodes cappadocica, 34
Ophiopogon planiscapus 'Nigrescens', 185
organic Viagra, 201
ornamental cherry, 175
ostrich fern, 25
over-wintering plants, 181, 186–187, 191, 217

Pagels, Ernst, 96
painted lady fern, 42
Papaver cambricum, 27, 34
Parrotia persica, 37
Pearson, Dan, 13, 187
Pépinières Delabroye, 189, 211
perennial honesty, 34
Perkins, Karen, 61, 76, 137, 218, 219
  cultivation tips of, 62, 77, 79
  on dividing epimediums, 190
Perraudière, Henri René le Tourneaux de la, 128, 200
Perry, Wendy, 129
Persian ironwood, 37
pests, 191–194
Plant Breeders' Rights, 209
Plant Delights Nursery, 125, 189, 218, 219
Plant Heritage, 221
Plant Hunters (nursery), 217
planting, 180
Pliny the Elder, 200
Podophyllum, 198
Podophyllum versipelle 'Spotty Dotty', 30
Polygonatum, 45
Polygonatum ×*hybridum*, 36, 37
Polystichum munitum, 36
Polystichum setiferum, 35, 36, 185
pots, 182–187
primroses, 32, 41
Primula vulgaris, 41
Probst, Darrell, 39, 77, 133, 164, 218, 219
  growing tips of, 134, 142, 189
  hybrids of, 73, 91, 116, 130, 137, 138, 145, 158
  on plant names, 143, 161, 208
  plants collected by, 50, 62, 109, 150, 202, 206, 219
  plants introduced by, 61, 88, 90, 100, 139, 149, 155, 165, 168

propagation
  by division, 190–191
  by seed, 188–190
Prunus, 175
Prunus serrula, 41
Prunus subhirtella 'Autumnalis', 41
Pulmonaria, 29, 30, 42
Pulmonaria 'Blue Ensign', 43, 187
Pyrus salicifolia var. *orientalis* 'Pendula', 41

rabbits, 193–194
rainwater, 179
randy beef grass, 200
Ranzania, 198
red barrenwort, 137
Reed, Matt, 216
rhizomes, 191
Rhododendron, 37
rhododendrons, 37, 39
RHS Flower Show, 221
RHS Garden Wisley, 14, 127, 178, 220
rodgersias, 24
Roscoea, 45
Roscoea purpurea 'Blackthorn Hybrid', 44
roses, 9, 176
rowan trees, 41
rowdy lamb herb, 200
Royal Botanic Gardens, Kew, 120, 202
Royal Horticultural Society, 127, 178, 220

Sackville-West, Vita, 41
Sanguinaria, 42, 199
Sanguinaria canadensis 'Flore Pleno', 218
Sarcococca, 32
Schenk, George, 142
scillas, 34, 185
sea holly, 156
seed pods, 182
seeds, 188–190
sequestered iron, 180
Sequestrene, 180

serviceberrry, 41
shade, finding and creating, 174–176
shield fern, 35, 36
shrubs, 9, 32, 34, 175–176
Siberian bugloss, 33
silver birch, 40
Sissinghurst, 41
smaller-flowered epimediums, 15–17
Smilacina, 199
Smilacina racemosa, 45
snowdrops, 38
snowy barrenwort, 167
soil, 36–39, 39, 174, 177–180
Solomon's seal, 36, 37
Sorbus, 41, 175
Spinners Garden and Nursery, 22, 110, 146
spreading epimediums, 32, 33, 182, 190, 221
  non-aggressively, 33, 34
spring bulbs, 9
Springer, Judy, 151
squills, 34
Stearn, William, 62, 71, 104, 153, 158, 206, 209, 212, 221
  plant identifications by, 120, 204–205
  plant names by, 83
Steinermema kraussei, 193
Stellaria media, 195
Strangman, Elizabeth, 7, 8, 21, 76, 166, 212
strawberry tree, 37
Sutton, Julian, 38, 112, 213
sweetgum, 37
Symphytum grandiflorum, 33
Syringa epimedium, 206

Tasmania, 217–218
tatarian dogwood, 26
Tiarella, 34
tiarellas, 185
Tobacco Mosaic Virus (TMV), 195
Tobacco Rattle Virus (TRV), 195
trees, 175–176

trilliums, 39, 43–44
trout lilies, 37
Tsūn-shen Ying, 205

United States, 218–220
U.S. National Arboretum, 133
Uvularia grandiflora, 45

Valentine, Betty, 164
Van Bogaert, Rik, 202, 203
Vancouveria, 198, 199, 205
van Noort, Marco, 122
Van Poucke, Koen, 94, 135, 212
Viagra, a natural form of, 200
Viburnum sieboldii, 25
Viburnum tinus, 28
Vicenza, Italy, 199
vine weevils, 191–193
viruses, 194–195
von Siebold, Philipp Franz, 85, 153, 201–202

Warley epimedium, 156
Warley Place, 156
Washfield Nursery, 7, 76
water, 179, 180, 184
Weaver, Dick, 92, 141
We Du Nursery, 90
weeping pear, 41
Welsh poppies, 27, 34
white-flowered bloodroot, 218
White, Robin, 109, 190, 202, 206, 214, 221
  hybrids of, 55, 57, 81, 82, 107, 131, 158, 209, 214
Wildside Nursery, 24, 42, 63, 106, 107, 214
Wiley, Keith, 39, 42, 214
  hybrids of, 26, 63, 64, 157, 215
Wiley, Ros, 214
Willmott, Ellen, 156
Wilson, George Fergusson, 127

winter colour, 59, 184
winter-flowering cherry, 41
Wirtz, Jacques, 212
witch hazel, 37
wood anemones, 32, 41–42
woodland perennials, 39
wood spurge, 33
Wudang Shan (Mount Wudang), 147, 206, 207
Wu Shan (Mount Wu), 160, 206

Yamaguchi's nursery, 111
year-round foliage, 29–30
Ying Tsün-shen, 160, 205
Ying Yang Huo, 200–201
Ypsilandra thibetica, 45, 186

ABOUT THE AUTHOR

SALLY GREGSON trained in nursery practice at Hadlow College in Kent, England, and then worked as a propagator in a small nursery specializing in acid-loving plants and perennials for flower arrangers. Following a move to Somerset, she set up her own nursery, Mill Cottage Plants, where she now concentrates on rare forms of hydrangeas and, increasingly, on epimediums.

When Sally first moved to Somerset, she inherited an empty 2.5-acre garden with very little shade. Over the past 25 years she has planted light trees, erected pergolas, and slowly created a more diverse landscape for her favourite shade-loving plants.

Epimediums have been one of her passions for more than 30 years. Some she has moved from Kent and replanted, but most of the new Chinese varieties have been acquired at the specialist plant sales she attends all over the United Kingdom.

Cover: *Epimedium* ×*versicolor* 'Neosulphureum'
Spine: *Epimedium* 'Pink Elf'
Title page: *Epimedium grandiflorum* 'Dark Beauty'.
Contents page: left to right, *Epimedium leptorrhizum* 'Mariko', *E. acuminatum*, and *E. campanulatum*.

Copyright © 2015 by Sally Gregson. All rights reserved.
Published in 2015 by Timber Press, Inc.

The Haseltine Building   6a Lonsdale Road
133 S.W. Second Avenue, Suite 450   London NW6 6RD
Portland, Oregon 97204-3527

For details on other Timber Press books and to sign up for our newsletters, please visit our websites, timberpress.com and timberpress.co.uk.

Library of Congress Cataloging-in-Publication Data
Gregson, Sally.
 The plant lover's guide to epimediums/Sally Gregson.—First edition.
     pages cm
 Includes index.
 ISBN 978-1-60469-475-8
 1. Epimedium. I. Title.
 QK495.B45G74 2015
 583'.34—dc23
                              2014024899

A catalogue record for this book is also available from the British Library.

Mention of trademark, proprietary product, or vendor does not constitute a guarantee or warranty of the product by the publisher or author and does not imply its approval to the exclusion of other products or vendors.

Book and cover design by Laken Wright
Layout and composition by Holly McGuire
Printed in China